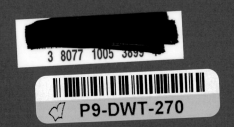

Twayne's English Authors Series

Sylvia E. Bowman, *Editor*

INDIANA UNIVERSITY

Arthur Hugh Clough

(TEAS) 97

Arthur Hugh Clough

By WENDELL V. HARRIS

University of Colorado

Twayne Publishers, Inc.   ::   New York

Preface

Arthur H. Clough's poetry has been the subject of a long series of reassessments beginning with the reviews of the posthumous *Poems* of 1862. Despite a majority verdict that Clough's poems are not quite first-rate, a considerable number of critics acquainted with his poetry have found it fascinating; and, dissatisfied with all previous valuations, one after another has tried to express what seemed to him a more just estimate. Almost all of Clough's critics have agreed on the importance of his poetry as an index to his age—uneasiness enters at the point where evaluation of its lasting poetic merit begins. Most of Clough's poems express his doubt about the relation between man, God, and the world; and it has been common to assume that his abandonment of poetry in middle life reflects his dismay at his inability to achieve a satisfactory resolution of his doubts. The defects of his poetry have been explained on the same theory: he is frequently seen as having been unable to perfect his art because he was unable to resolve the tensions existing within his mind.

I believe that Clough was finally successful in accommodating himself to, if not in wholly mastering, his doubts, and that he is frequently impressive as a poet. Moreover, it seems to me important to recognize that he very frequently used poetry as a means of clarifying his speculations. His poetry was the sound of hammer on anvil as he attempted to shape answers. When he had finally beaten out a form of belief he could accept, the intellectual forge cooled and the anvil ceased to ring. The forms of Clough's doubts, and the results of his efforts to come to terms with them, can be traced clearly in his poems and essays. Since the stages in his thought do not correspond altogether with the major events of his life, I have placed in the first chapter the biographical facts, together with a brief consideration of the currents of thought which had the most influence on him, thus clearing the way for concentration on his poetry. I have devoted a chapter each to *The Bothie of Tober-na-Vuolich, Amours de Voyage,* and *Dipsychus,* his three longest poems, and one to *Ambarvalia,* the collection of shorter poems from his Oxford days. The four works reflect, though each in a different way, a series of doubts, intellectual struggles, and attempted resolutions. The position in which Clough finally found comparative psychological and intellectual comfort is presented through an examination of the shorter poems written after he left Oxford and of his prose, the subjects of chapters six and seven. His last poetic effort, *Mari Magno,* is treated in a brief chapter, and a summary view of Clough's relationship to Matthew Arnold and of the significance of his poetry from the point of view of the twentieth century closes the volume.

Much of Clough's poetry was published only after his death, and thus in many cases editorial choices must be made among the variant readings scattered through many and often imperfect manuscripts. The problem has been additionally complicated by uncertainty as to whether some of the omissions, choices of readings, and additions of titles in the editions supervised by Mrs. Clough were based on the poet's wishes as known to her alone. The Oxford edition of the poems, as pointed out in a very important article by Richard Gollin, has not been entirely consistent in the treatment of these matters, and has omitted a number of poems, passages, and variant readings.[1] It is nevertheless the most reliable edition of Clough's poems we have and, if Mr. Gollin's strictures are kept in mind, a most helpful one. I have therefore used its readings in almost every case. I have also cited Clough's poems in accordance with the titles there given them. Untitled poems have been treated in the usual way: the first four or five words of the first line have been used, the initial letter of the first word only being capitalized. I have cited Clough's notebooks according to their description in the Oxford *Poems;* and, where quoting from the longer poems, I have included in parentheses the pages of that edition on which the quoted lines appear.

M. Paul Veyriras' study of Clough came to hand as I was completing the writing of this volume; Professor Michael Timko's *Innocent Victorian* appeared several months after I had submitted the text to the editor of Twayne's English Authors Series.

I found that in several cases I had labored to make points quite similar to ones expressed in one or the other of these studies. However, since I approached these points in a different way, I decided to allow these portions of my treatment to stand rather than to abbreviate them and cite Veyriras and Timko.

I have tried to avoid cluttering the text with minor points and unnecessary references; the rather full notes to each chapter should lead the interested reader to more ample discussions of the most important of those matters I felt it unnecessary to discuss in detail.

Acknowledgments

Together with all other students of Clough, I am in debt to the editors of the Oxford *Poems* (Professors H. F. Lowry, A. L. P. Norrington, and F. L. Mulhauser), and additionally to Professor Mulhauser for his well-edited edition of Clough's correspondence.

I wish to acknowledge my gratitude to the Keeper of Western Manuscripts of the Bodleian Library for permission to consult the Clough manuscripts under his care and to quote from previously unpublished portions of these, to Miss Margaret Crum of the Bodleian for very kindly correcting an inaccurate transcription from the manuscripts, and to Miss Katharine Duff for permission to quote from Clough's unpublished letters and papers.

I should also like to thank the following publishers: the Clarendon Press, Oxford, for permission to quote extensively from *The Correspondence of Arthur Hugh Clough*, edited by F. L. Mulhauser (1957), *The Letters of Matthew Arnold to Arthur Hugh Clough*, edited by H. F. Lowry (1932), and *The Poems of Arthur Hugh Clough*, edited by H. F. Lowry, A. L. P. Norrington, and F. L. Mulhauser (1951); the University of Alabama Press for permission to quote equally extensively from *Selected Prose Works of Arthur Hugh Clough*, edited by Buckner Trawick (1964); and Doubleday and Company, Inc., for permission to quote form *Goethe's Faust*, translated by Walter Kaufmann (1961).

Finally, I wish to express my very real appreciation to the Council on Research and Creative Work of the University of Colorado, both for the Faculty Fellowship which enabled me to write this book, and their generosity in meeting many of the inevitable expenses of preparing it for publication.

Contents

Chronology

1819   Arthur Hugh Clough born on January 1; second son of James Butler Clough and Anne, née Perfect.

1822   The Clough family moves from Liverpool to Charleston, South Carolina.

1828   Arthur brought back to England for his schooling; enters a preparatory school at Chester.

1829   Enters Rugby where Dr. Thomas Arnold is newly headmaster.

1835   Clough editor of the *Rugby Magazine;* named head of the School House.

1836   Wins Balliol Scholarship.

1837   Enters Balliol College, Oxford.

1841   Takes second-class degree in the Oxford Schools Examination.

1842   After failing to obtain a Fellowship at Balliol, Clough elected a Fellow of Oriel. Beginning of close friendship with Matthew and Tom Arnold.

1847   Leads reading part to Scotland; finds inspiration for the *Bothie.*

1848   Resigns tutorship in January; to Paris in May; resigns Oriel Fellowship in October; brings out the *Bothie* in November.

1849   *Ambarvalia* published in January. Takes holiday in Italy in the spring, remains in Rome during French siege against Mazzini Republic; writes *Amours;* assumes duties at University Hall, London.

1850   Autumn holiday in Venice where *Dipsychus* begun.

1851   Meets Blanche Smith.

1852   Resigns as principal of University Hall; announces engagement; sails for America at the end of October.

1853   Returns to England; assumes duties as examiner in the Education Office in July.

1854 Marriage to Blanche Smith in June.
1857 Begins attending to editorial and other duties for Florence Nightingale.
1858 Publication of *Amours* in *Atlantic Monthly*.
1859 Publication of Clough's revision of Dryden's version of *Plutarch's Lives*.
1860 Clough's health begins to fail.
1861 Travels to Greece, Constantinople, France, Switzerland, and Italy; begins *Mari Magno*; dies November 13 in Florence.
1862 Publication of *Poems of Arthur Hugh Clough,* edited by Blanche Clough.

CHAPTER 1

Clough in Context

CONTEMPORARY reviews of that portion of Clough's poetry published during his lifetime concerned themselves primarily with the amount of promise shown by his work; most subsequent essays on Clough, whether biographical or critical, have been devoted to discussing why Clough did not fulfill more of that promise, and, as a corollary, have debated whether either his life or his poetry can be regarded as successful. Actually, few have ever directly argued, in print, that he was a failure. But—as the list of Clough's defenders has grown, each beginning with the assumption that Clough is in great need of defense—it has become clear that even his partisans do not regard each other as especially convincing. The defenses have been, for the most part, divisible into two arguments: that Clough was a successful poet but unsuccessful as the man of action he wished to be; or alternatively, that, while not very impressive as a poet, Clough achieved the rare distinction of being a man of entire intellectual honesty. The two positions clearly stand in each other's way, the tendency having unfortunately been for each to cancel the other and thus to reinforce the negative conclusion that Clough was indeed, in one way or another, a failure.

The matter has been additionally complicated by the attempts to explain *why* Clough did not accomplish more. His mother's rigorous moral teaching; his isolation from his family when sent from Charlestown, South Carolina, to England for his education; the hyper-earnest atmosphere of Rugby under Dr. Arnold; the religious turmoil generated by his Oxford tutor, W. G. Ward; and the uninspiring curriculum of the Oxford of the time—all these have received blame for Clough's second-class degree and for the doubt and indecisiveness which seemed to plague him for the rest of his life. Dr. Arnold has received the greatest share of this blame, but even here there is fairly wide disagreement since estimates of the degree of Arnold's culpability tend to shade off into evaluation of the total effect on English education of Arnold's headmastership at Rugby. Another favorite topic for scholarly debate has been the relationship between Clough and Matthew Arnold. The friendship between the two was for a considerable time extremely close; the letters from Arnold to Clough are an important source of information about both men; Arnold's great elegy, "Thyrsis," is one reason that Clough's name is as well known as it is. But comparisons of the two men have tended to become invidious, going beyond the careful discrimination of differences to the use of one as a foil to the other.

I shall attempt to avoid any evaluation of Clough's life—when we talk about whether a man is "successful," we are imposing arbitrarily chosen criteria even in employing standards generally agreed upon within our own culture and time. We cannot know finally and certainly the degree of happiness or unhappiness, of hope or despair, felt by Clough or by any other man at any particular period of his life, not even where there exist letters and personal statements to help.

On the other hand, to consider the degree to which a man achieved his announced practical goals and to analyze the external obstacles which confronted him is, of course, possible; and this I shall necessarily do. Similarly, rather than argue the success or failure of Clough's poetry or try to determine what part of it belongs to the first, second, or third rank, I shall, while pointing out from time to time both faults and achievements, try simply to show why it is worthy of attention.

I   An Age in Ferment

Clough's poems have long been regarded as of special interest for the very vivid picture they present of the intellectual perplexities worrying at the minds of educated and thoughtful Victorians. The well-known comment of James Russell Lowell has proved accurate: "I have a foreboding that Clough, imperfect as he was in many respects, and dying before he had subdued his sensitive temperament to the sterner requirements of his art, will be thought a hundred years hence to have been the truest expression in verse of the moral and intellectual tendencies, the doubt and struggle towards settled convictions, of the period in which he lived." [1]

It is necessary to pause for a moment over the specific historical controversies which generated in Clough's time a sequence of questions leading back and back to first principles. Though speculation about evolution was already occurring among the informed some years before the publication of Darwin's *Origin of Species* (1859), the reconciliation of the claims of science and religion does not appear to have been a problem for Clough and his friends.[2] The results of the German "Higher Criticism" which were filtering through to England were more disturbing. But neither were D. F. Strauss or his fellow-laborers the main source of the painful religious questioning of the 1830's and 1840's. Had Benjamin Jowett's highly controversial "On the Interpretation of Scripture" appeared in print as early as Clough's undergraduate career, neither he nor his circle would have been shocked. Rather, the central question which set off so much soul-searching was in the first instance a deceptively simple doctrinal one: "What is the Church of England?" That question naturally resolved itself into a more specific one, "What are the grounds of the authority of the Church of England?"

These questions were generated by the state of the Church at the time. Its vitality had once again ebbed following the decline of the Evangelical movement,[3] and the clamor from without for reform was running so high that many of those churchmen who felt most strongly the need for a revitalization of the Church feared its excess. The repeal of the Test Act in 1828, and the Catholic emancipation of 1829 were regarded by many as threatening; the alarm was increased by the Reform Bill of 1832, which gave political power to a class not strongly disposed to support the Established Church. The controversy over the reform of the universities was necessarily closely allied with that over the Church since reformers wished to lessen the Anglican character of those institutions by abolishing the requirement that all students subscribe to the XXXIX Articles of Religion at matriculation.

It was in this atmosphere that the bill to suppress ten Anglican bishoprics in Ireland was introduced and subsequently passed, giving the occasion for John Keble's sermon on "National Apostasy" which is generally taken as opening the Oxford Movement. The sermon, delivered at Oxford in St. Mary's Church on July 14, 1833, protested against the principle "that the Apostolical Church in this realm is henceforth only to stand, in the eye of the State, *as one sect among many,* depending for any pre-eminence she may still appear to retain, merely upon the accident of her having a strong party in the country." [4] The first of the series of Oxford Tracts which followed, written by John Henry Newman and bearing the date September 9, 1833, was focused, naturally enough, on the sources of the authority of the ministers of the Church of England. Its argument was direct: "we have neglected the real ground on which our authority is built—OUR APOSTOLICAL DESCENT." [5]

The battle lines within the Church were now clearly drawn, for such a position was in direct conflict with the endeavors of the Anglican Liberals to strengthen the Church by broadening her doctrines and, insofar as possible, by removing the doctrinal barriers between her and the dissenting churches. The struggle which thus came about led some men from an examination of the source of the authority of the Church of England to a scepticism about the truth of Christianity, led others to find adequate authority for the Christian Church only in Roman Catholicism, and caused many among those who remained orthodox Anglicans some years of anxious questioning. Clough's writings record a long personal search for a sure ground of religious belief—a search which had been initiated by the widespread controversy over the authority and sufficiency of the doctrines of the Church of England.

They also betray his concern for a socially just and economically sane social structure. A thoughtful and conscientious man of the time could hardly have ignored the misery of much of the working class and the need for political, economic, and social reforms. It had begun to dawn on the country that perhaps it could afford to allow factory workers a seventy-two-hour week and their children a forty-eight-hour week leavened with a few hours of schooling. G. M. Young has pointed out how much impetus the combined forces of Evangelicanism and Utilitarianism had given to the examination and rectification of some of the most obvious offences against England's conscience, but evidence of the need for reform was appearing much faster than widespread hostility and apathy would allow reforms to be undertaken.[6] During the 1830's, parliamentary commissions were producing mountains of highly damning statistics about the state of the poor in England; the aspect of these statistics was not improved by the depression which began in the latter part of the decade. By 1842, the year

Clough was awarded his tutorship at Oriel, Thomas Carlyle, Charles Dickens, and the seventh Earl of Shaftesbury had all, in their various ways, made eloquent protests against the inhumanity and stupidity of the social order, and the Chartist unrest had impressed the point on many who read neither literature nor parliamentary reports.

Neither Clough nor his friends and immediate mentors announced adherence to any specific scheme for refurbishing the social fabric of England, and therefore it is easy to overlook their dismay at its manifold imperfections. There is considerable evidence, however, that they were strongly affected by the recognition of the amount of remediable evil around them. Thomas Arnold, Dr. Arnold's son and one of Clough's closest friends, was speaking of economic evils as much as ecclesiastical turmoil when he gave his view of England in a letter to Clough in 1847:

> Those are indeed happy who can still hope for England, who can find, in identifying themselves with our political or social institutions, a congenial atmosphere; and a suitable machinery for accomplishing at last all that they dream of. Of such sanguine spirits, alas! I am not one. To imagine oneself called upon to "do good," in the age in which we live, is an illusion to which I was long subject myself, but of the utter fallaciousness of which I am now convinced.[7]

Clough was less pessimistic about the state of England than Thomas Arnold, but he, like many other Victorians, shared his misgivings.

In addition to the clarity with which he reflects the intellectual searching of his age, Clough's work makes two other claims on our interest. First, the poetically intensified report of intellectual conflict to be found there is a valuable example of intellectual honesty amidst perplexities still unresolved; and, second, Clough did finally arrive at a resolution. The search for a more durable spiritual or intellectual armor to replace that form of Christianity which was so badly hacked and battered in the latter part of the nineteenth century still goes on. The terms of debate change, but the difficulties faced are not so different today from those Clough faced now more than a hundred years ago. Moreover, the problems Clough explores are, underneath their especially Victorian form, basic human problems which have vexed men in all ages. In the most radical form they are simply *What is Truth?* and *What is the Good?* Clough throws the complexities attending these eternal riddles into relief while rejecting all easy factitious answers.

We have inherited the Victorians' doubt and struggle toward a "settled conviction" and developed that legacy into a skepticism deeper, wider, and more cynical. The "Sea of Faith" has now receded so far out of sight and hearing that many of us can hardly conceive what it must have been, and we therefore mistake the puddles of conventional religious observance for the sea that once lapped a whole culture. Matthew Arnold's naked shingles having become T. S. Eliot's wasteland, the artists most honored, at least by the more sophisticated, are those who portray the dryness or absurdity of the terrain on which they feel man now lives.

Clough saw the same uncertainty as the twentieth-century writers but he does not, as they have too often done, project the confusion of his own mind on the outer world and then go on to theorize about how to live in the world he has thus constructed. That is, he does not, for instance, say: "My mind encounters absurdities when it tries to find meaning or direction in life and therefore life *is* absurd, and all that remains is to theorize about how to live in that absurdity." Rather, in all his questioning, he tries simply to report faithfully the processes of his own mind. From Clough's point of view the world *may* be absurd or hostile or meaningless; but he can't *know* that any more than he can *know* that our life is structured by the grand design of a benevolent God. There is an honesty in this position which should still have value and interest, and perhaps a corrective power, in the twentieth century. Nor did Clough despair because of the difficulty of discovering the truth of things—that truth might never be humanly attainable daunted him but little.

> It fortifies my soul to know
> That, though I perish, Truth is so:
> That, howso'er I stray and range,
> Whate'er I do, Thou dost not change.
> I steadier step when I recall
> That, if I slip, Thou dost not fall.[8]

Neither early, when he hoped to achieve some degree of insight into the "truth" of man's existence, or later, when he became convinced of the impossibility of seeing whatever overall plan there might be, did he fail to find comfort in the belief that "Truth is so."

Clough did arrive at a position in which he could rest. Many of the poems written in the years 1849–52, when Clough was at the height of his poetic activity, express a more bracing and hopeful view of life than has hitherto been recognized; indeed, they represent a kind of resolution to the problems explored in his earlier poetry. This, like all other interpretations of the content of Clough's poetry here offered, is grounded in the first instance in a reading of the poems themselves. Where biographical or historical information clarifies a poem or prevents its misreading, I have, of course, taken cognizance of it; but I have attempted to avoid the risky procedure of using biographical information to extrapolate the poet's thought beyond what is expressed in the poetry, just as I have tried to resist the temptation to use isolated extracts from the poems to fill in where biographical information is scarce.

In the process of presenting this reading of Clough's poetry, I will have occasion to reinterpret to some extent the usual view of Clough's attitude toward life at various states of his career. I do not believe that when Clough immersed himself in domestic responsibilities and routine work after his marriage, he was trying to escape from doubts and speculations whose pressure had become overwhelming. Rather, it seems to me that in the years just before his marriage, Clough arrived at a position which satisfied him, and that he ceased to write poetry at least partly because for him it was the vehicle of his speculations, one now no longer needed.

One of Clough's essays, written just after the period he had passed through his final intellectual crisis, advances at least half-seriously the theory that literary creations embody not the ripest wisdom of the writer but positions he must discard as his mind moves on. "The Iliad is but the scum of the mind of Homer, and Plato's dialogues the refuse of his thought." [9] Admitting the exaggeration of this statement when applied to the great writers of the past, Clough wonders if it is not perhaps true of the writers of the modern age. It would seem at least to be true of himself; Clough often followed one poem by another stating a contradictory view as though to remove the conflict from his mind to the page and thus acquire perspective in regard to it. When at last the conflict was resolved, he ceased to write poetry until, at the end of his life, he wrote the conventional and largely uninteresting *Mari Magno*.

II *Clough's Early Years*

Five full-scale literary biographies of Clough exist; since 1962 the standard treatment has been that by Lady Katharine Chorley, though its pre-eminence has been challenged by Paul Veyriras' recent study.[10] Despite differences of interpretation and the availability of a greater number of letters and other documents in late years, the essential facts and interpretations have been little altered by the later biographers from those to be found in the "Memoir" published in the *Poems and Prose Remains* of 1869,[11] written very largely, if not entirely, by Mrs. Clough, and Leslie Stephen's account in the *Dictionary of Natural Biography* (1887).

Mrs. Clough's account is especially valuable: though naturally it attempts to present Clough's life in the best possible light, it is the source for a great many facts and quotations which later biographers have heavily relied upon, and her interpretations of the influences on Clough's life represent the major themes around which later writers have woven variations. However, neither she nor later writers have perceived the sequence of changes which lies behind Clough's successive periods. It is important to realize this, for it explains partially why Clough's life and poetry are accorded such similar interpretations even by writers who strongly disagree in their final evaluation of Clough's importance.

Clough was born on January 1, 1819, the second son of James Clough, a Liverpool cotton merchant descended from a line of English country gentlemen with estates in Wales, and the former Anne Perfect, the daughter of a Pontefract banker. The family moved to Charlestown in the winter of 1822–23 to improve the father's business prospects, but in 1828 Arthur Hugh was taken to England for his education. After a time in a preparatory school in Chester, he entered Rugby in the fall of 1829, a year after the appointment of Dr. Arnold as headmaster. Accumulating academic honors and prestige among his peers, winning the only scholarship open to those under fourteen, becoming head of the fifth form at fifteen, making something of a name as an athlete, and editing the Rugby magazine, Clough achieved high distinction in the school. The lofty idealism which Mrs. Clough imparted to her children and especially, according to family accounts, to Arthur Hugh was met at least halfway by Dr. Arnold's effort to transmit a high moral purpose to his pupils. Heroes and martyrs had been Mrs. Clough's favorite subjects in reading to Arthur; the enormous consequences of the slightest misstep was Dr. Arnold's constant subject in his sermons at Rugby.

Dr. Arnold's system depended heavily on the sixth form "praeposters" to keep order and set the moral tone of the school, and Clough's schoolboy letters show him totally involved in his responsibilities as a leader even before his entry into the sixth form. Perhaps the best illustration of this seriousness is the prayer for the success of the Rugby magazine that Professor Lowry transcribed from one of Clough's Rugby journals. It begins:

> O all-wise God, whose Providence has ordained this undertaking, and laid its weight on me, grant that it be not a snare unto me. Let it not interfere with those more especial duties which I am placed here to perform,—with my efforts to improve myself in knowledge and intellectual power so as to be better fit for the duties of my future life,—far less with those I should ever be making for my own spiritual improvement, and that of my companions. Spacious Father, give me thy Holy Spirit whilst I am busied in this work, that neither by the sense of intellectual power or the praises of others my foolish and wicked vanity be excited in me.[12]

The later effects of the adulation of Dr. Arnold which inspired Clough to become the model schoolboy are difficult to evaluate. Many critics have commented on the adverse effects of the Rugby experience on Clough's poetry. James I. Osborne's study, published in 1920, summed up Arnold's influence by saying that it narrowed Clough's outlook to the point that "Connections which youthful intuition might have taken in at a glance, if given the opportunity, he was later compelled to puzzle out at vast expense of middle-age reasoning." [13] Humbert Wolfe, in an essay of 1932, charged Arnold with having overstrained Clough's sensibilities in a way that was permanently damaging.[14] It is easy to blame Clough's extreme conscientiousness on a too-ready acceptance of Arnold's precepts, especially when one reads through Dr. Arnold's *Sermons Preached in the Chapel of Rugby School* and comes across such sermons as the eighth[15] in which the schoolboys who tempt their fellows into idleness or extravagance are told not only that they sin, but that they may apply directly to themselves Matthew XVIII:6, "Whoso shall offend one of these little ones which believe in me, it were better for him that a millstone were hanged around his neck, and that he were drowned in the depth of the sea."

But, after all, Arnold's sermons were perfectly orthodox, and where he departed from the beliefs of the majority of Anglican clergymen, it was on the side of doctrinal liberalism. There is nothing in the sermons to compare with the specimen of a Jesuit school sermon that James Joyce has given us in *Portrait of an Artist*, and nothing which could not have been heard from many an English pulpit. The force of his personality and the peculiar earnestness of his character must have made his preaching unusually effective, so much so that he may not have known how great an effect he was producing. Such an underestimation of his own effectiveness is perhaps what Clough had in mind when he later referred to Arnold as one "too fit to head armies and to rule kingdoms to succeed in weighing words and analyzing emotions; born to do, they know not what to do." [16] We know from Clough's letters that he valued Arnold's sermons and continued to find nourishment in them,[17] and certain correspondences between Arnold's sermons and some of Clough's poems stand out plainly. But the exact assessment of one man's influence on another is a very difficult task; and, as Professor Winchester suggested in a balanced and sympathetic essay, the conscientiousness with which Clough pursued his goals, one of them certainty of belief, seems an essential part of his personality, not merely an attitude engrafted by another.[18]

In any case, Clough's tendency toward an almost morbidly painful self-analysis was already showing itself while he was at Rugby. The scrupulous analysis of his own motives and thoughts has often been assumed a product of his Oxford days, but it appears much earlier in his letters. One such passage occurs in a letter written to his mother in 1835.

I was in a very queer humour, when I wrote the 2 pages preceding this [written 11 days earlier], at least so it seems to me now after reading them over again. I wish I could get rid of this humour-rule, but there are times when I feel so utterly weak both in intellectual and moral power that I half fancy myself crazed. Again there are other times when I feel so strong that I could do anything; and then I can look back and judge rightly of what is past. . . . But I must take care now also, and stop this talk, for egotizing comme ça is very exciting indeed, and I begin to feel my face getting hot and my mind confused. . . . I am half sorry I wrote this, but I felt so strong and healthy when [I] began this page that I thought I could tell you all about myself, etc., bu[t] I soon got muddled; and after all I believe that the excess of thinking about one's self is very ruinous indeed.[19]

A letter to Simpkinson from 1836 in which Clough tries to explain his precise feelings about his Rugby acquaintances provides another excellent example of this painstaking self-analysis.[20] But, on the other hand, there is also plenty of evidence in the Rugby magazine of Clough's boyish good spirits and normal adolescent levity.

III   *The Oxford Years*

Holding a Balliol scholarship, Clough went up to Oxford in October, 1837. Since rather too little is known of Clough's life at Oxford for one to be entirely sure of the university's effect on him, more has been made of certain bits of information and firsthand comments from this time than these perhaps deserve. For instance, Clough seems to have lived a somewhat ascetic life at Oxford, attending few social gatherings and working in a cold, fireless room; but it is impossible to know how much of this mode of life was self-imposed as a kind of discipline and how much was due to the simple lack of funds. A letter quoted in the "Memoir" gives warrant for both interpretations: W. G. Ward reported that Clough "told me that his pecuniary circumstances incapacitated him from giving wine parties, and that therefore he did not like to wine with others." [21] But Ward then attributes Clough's reserve to "a certain fastidiousness of taste and judgment"; and Clough is also reported to have said, with what degree of irony it is now impossible to determine, that working in cold rooms was excellent for keeping out visitors.[22]

Similarly, much has been made of a comment of Clough's recorded by Frederick Temple: "When I am talking to Ward, I feel like a bit of paper blown up the chimney by a draught, and one doesn't always like being a bit of paper;—so I sometimes keep away from the draught." [23] Quoted in full, the comment does betray Clough's feeling that he is swept off balance by theological discussion with Ward, but it includes the common-sense resolution to avoid being too often subject to the experience. It is inaccurate, therefore, simply to state, as many have done, that Clough felt like "a straw drawn up the chimney" in the midst of the Oxford controversy—that clearly is putting the thing too strongly.

In the same way the following passage from a letter to Simpkinson, frequently quoted as evidence that contact with Ward was disturbing, also shows that Clough's analytical mind gave him a degree of critical objectivity: "I only hope to escape the vortex of Philosophism and Discussion, (whereof Ward is the Centre), as it is the most exhausting exercise in the world. . . . It seems to have a different effect on Stanley and Lake, but I do not think it can be wholly beneficial to anyone." [24] Nor was Ward clearly the dominant personality in the relationship; in fact, his letters to Clough betray an almost neurotic dependence on Clough's friendship.[25] Such a relationship may very well not have been comfortable or even entirely healthy for Clough, but it is unlikely that he was simply swept against his will into intellectual swamps by a stronger personality.

In any case, Clough could hardly have avoided the expenditure of considerable thought and intellectual energy on the theological battles of the time. The Oxford Movement had arisen four years before Clough entered Oxford, but Newman's famous Tract Ninety, which was to confirm the worst fears of those who had seen Rome at the end of the Tractarian road, lay still four years in the future. The central teaching of the Oxford Movement, that the true ground of the authority of the Church was the "apostolical descent," was so directly opposed to those of the liberal element of the Anglican Church, of which Dr. Arnold was a leader, that Arnold had in April, 1836, published a strong attack on the Oxford Movement under the title (apparently not his own) "The Oxford Malignants." [26] With his devotion to Arnold on the one hand, and the influence carried by Newman's powerful sermons on the other, Clough could hardly have avoided an inner debate over the issues being raised even had the Tractarian Ward not been his tutor and friend.

In addition, both James Osborne and Lady Katharine Chorley have emphasized in their biographies the enervating effect of the monotonously narrow curriculum at Oxford on such a student as Clough, who had come from Rugby with a solid background already acquired in the studies offered and with a sense of responsibility for which there was no outlet. Whether these causes adequately explain the outcome we shall now never know, but all who knew Clough were shocked when in the spring of 1841, instead of brilliantly capping his academic career, he took a Second Class.

Clough was further disappointed by his failure to achieve a Balliol Fellowship, but he retrieved his position with the receipt of a Fellowship at Oriel College in 1842. The succeeding few years seem to have constituted a period of unusual happiness for Clough. Matthew Arnold came up to Oxford in 1841, and his young brother Tom in 1842; it is from this time that their close friendship dates. The Arnold brothers and Theodore Walrond, also from Rugby, constituted with Clough a most congenial group. With the two Arnolds Clough also became a member of the Decade, the intellectually exclusive debating society that included Benjamin Jowett, F. T. Palgrave, Arthur Stanley, and J. C. Shairp. These first years at Oriel passed pleasantly, with Clough much in the company of the two Arnolds and Walrond, breakfasting with them on Sunday mornings, dining out, and going on long walks and boating expeditions with them. Clough's letters take on a different tone in these years, for though he and his friends continue to discuss serious issues, the whole mood of the correspondence is sunnier.

Clough seems also to have very much enjoyed leading parties to the Lake District and Scotland. But beneath the congenial surface of his life at Oxford an inner turmoil was building up, concentrated around Clough's feelings toward the XXXIX Articles of the Anglican Church, the stumbling block for many conscientious men of the time. Clough signed the articles in the fall of 1843, a necessity if he were to be appointed as a permanent tutor; but the doubts he had felt about being able to subscribe without reservations to the articles continued to grow, while looming in the future were the Holy Orders he would have to take (within six years of his M.A. by College Statutes) if he were to remain at Oxford. Already by the spring of 1846 he was writing to his sister Anne that "my fellowship will end, I suppose, in June '49." [27]

We have the testimony of Thomas Arnold that Clough had been actively following the "higher criticism" of the German scholars and finding the position taken by David Friedrich Strauss much more amenable to reason than the XXXIX Articles.[28] Strauss, analyzing the New Testament from a historical point of view, had reached the conclusion that the amount of historical fact to be discovered under the mythological accretions which make up some of the Biblical accounts of Jesus was small indeed. He does not doubt that Jesus represents the ideal for man; but, "though we cannot conceive of it [the ideal] as existing otherwise than under the form of a perfect man, and though it is not impossible that such a man may have lived, as we are all intended to resemble this ideal, still it is not necessary that we should know of the existence of such a man or believe in it, but solely that we should keep that ideal before us, recognize it as obligatory on us, and strive to make ourselves like it." [29] (Arnold's "The Better Part" presents essentially the same position though with emphasis on the affirmation which replaces the earlier belief.)

The exact extent to which Clough accepted Strauss's position at this time is open to question, but even partial assent was of course incompatible with the XXXIX Articles. Feeling it to be distasteful to examine deeply his own attitudes to each of the Articles and finding it impossible any longer to seem to believe what he was no longer sure could be believed, he resigned his tutorship as of Easter, 1848, and his Fellowship in the fall of that year. He outlined the fruit of his speculations at the time in a letter to his sister Anne in May, 1847:

. . . I cannot feel sure that a man may not have all that is important in Christianity even if he does not so much as know that Jesus of Nazareth existed. . . . Trust in God's Justice and Love, and belief in his Commands as written in our Conscience stand unshaken, though Matthew, Mark, Luke, and John or even St. Paul, were to fall. The thing which men must work at, will not be critical questions about the scriptures, but philosophical problems of Grace and Free Will, and of the Redemption as an Idea, not as an historical event. What is the meaning of 'Atonement by a crucified Saviour'?—*How* many of the Evangelicals can answer that?—

That there may be meaning in it . . . I don't deny;—but I do deny that Mr. McNeile or Mr. Close, or Dr. Hook, or Pusey, or Newman himself quite know what to make of it: the Evangelicals gabble at it, as the Papists do their Ave Mary's—and yet say they know; while Newman falls down and worships *because* he does not know and knows he does not know.

I think others are more right, who say boldly, We don't understand it, and therefore we *won't* fall down and worship it. Though there is no occasion for adding—'there *is* nothing in it—' I should say, Until I know, I will wait: and if I am not born with the power to discover, I will do what I can, with what knowledge I have. . . .[30]

During the lengthy correspondence carried on with the Provost of Oriel, Edward Hawkins, Clough explained, in answer to a question from Hawkins, the kind of religious problems he felt that he and many other men of his generation were facing:

. . . I think there is a general feeling that Miracles are poor proofs. The doctrine must prove them, not they the doctrine. Can we be sure that anything is really a miracle? . . . Again books like Strauss's life of Jesus have disturbed the historical foundations of Christianity. And people ask further what has History to do with Religion? The worth of such a doctrine as that of the Holy Ghost as the Lord and Giver of spiritual life is intelligible: but what is the value of biographical facts? —External evidence is slighted: but I think the great query is rather as to the *internal* evidence. Is Xtianity really so much better than Mohometanism, Buddhism (a more extensive faith) or the old heathen philosophy?[31]

Additional light on Clough's position at this time is revealed by a letter to Clough dated August 18, 1848, in which Tom Arnold refers to "what we call superstition; that is to say . . . a belief in a particular Providence and in visitation and warnings from the unseen world." [32]

However, important as it was in his life, there has been a tendency to overemphasize Clough's religious questioning during his time at Oxford and to concentrate too much on the influence first of Dr. Arnold and then of the Tractarians in producing the mental conflicts of these years. Perhaps equally important during the 1840's—and throughout the rest of his life—was the influence of Thomas Carlyle. Clough was strongly influenced by Carlyle's writing long before they met. *Sartor Resartus* had first appeared in *Fraser's Magazine* in 1833–34, *Heroes, Hero-Worship and the Heroic in History* in 1841, and *Past and Present* in 1843. There was a strong interest in Carlyle among Clough's Oxford circle in the early 1840's, and evidence of Carlyle's influence begins to appear soon after in Clough's writing.

The circumstances of their first meeting are unknown (Lady Chorley assigns it to "1847, or earlier" [33]), and it would indeed be

of great interest to know more about the whole course of their
friendship than is at present discoverable. Unlike as the prophet
of the Everlasting Yea and the painfully conscientious poet would
seem, there were strong grounds for mutual appreciation. The
elder man's regard was exceptional: according to Jowett he
thought Clough "the most high-principled man he had ever
known." [34] That Carlyle would have been able to understand and
sympathize with the young poet is suggested by a number of passages in Carlyle's major works which reveal an understanding of
men like Clough. For instance, in the opening pages of *Heroes
and Hero-Worship* Carlyle is at pains to insist that "a man's religion is the chief fact with regard to him" so long as religion is
defined not as an accepted creed but as a man's working out of his
own beliefs:

> But the thing a man does practically believe . . . the thing a man
> does practically lay to heart, and know for certain, concerning his vital
> relations to this mysterious Universe, and his duty and destiny there,
> that is in all cases the primary thing for him, and creatively determines
> all the rest. This is his *religion;* or, it may be, his mere scepticism and
> *no-religion:* the manner it is in which he feels himself to be spiritually
> related to the Unseen World or No-World. . . .[35]

There are affinities in matters much more personal. Clough's
delight in bathing in cold streams and the feeling he seems to
have had about its spiritual effect have been described by many
who knew him; a biographer comments that at one period
"Clough's soul seems to have demanded for its good a November
series of daily plunges." [36] That was an attitude Carlyle shared:
"What Worship, for example, is there not in mere Washing! Perhaps one of the most moral things a man, in common cases, has it
in his power to do. Strip thyself, go into the bath, or were it into
the limpid pool and running brook, and there wash and be clean;
thou wilt step out again a purer and better man." [37]

Carlyle's influence on Clough's style is obvious, appearing, for
instance, in his letters to his friends, which become increasingly
figurative and allusive from the middle of the 1840's. Thus the
opening of a letter to Stanley in 1848 could have come directly
from the pages of *Past and Present:* "Ichabod, Ichabod, the glory
is departed. Liberty, Equality, and Fraternity, driven back by

shopkeeping bayonet, hides her red cap in dingiest St. Antoine. Well-to-do-ism shakes her Egyptian scourge to the tune of Ye are idle, ye are idle; the tale of bricks will be doubled, and Moses and Aaron of Socialism can at best only pray for plagues. . . ." [38] Many of Carlyle's central beliefs find their way into Clough's writing at about the same time. Clough's Oxford Retrenchment Pamphlet of 1847 bases itself on the argument that "Ultimately it is the earth that forms our wealth and subsistence" and thus "for meat and drink and all things there is one sole machine, not made with hands, not capable of duplication, this terraqueous globe that moves incommunicably tied to one unchanging orbit," as given to man by God. [39] That point need not necessarily, of course, have been taken from Carlyle; but the resemblance to the argument of Chapter VIII of Book III of *Past and Present* is striking: "Properly speaking, the land belongs to these two: To the Almighty God; and to all His Children of Men that have ever worked well on it."

And in his poetry when Clough is at his most optimistic, as in passages of the *Bothie,* Carlyle's similar affirmations can generally be heard echoing beneath the surface. The influence of Carlyle and the sense of kinship between the two men explains many of Clough's early intellectual positions. The answers provided by Carlyle were modified by Clough, but in accepting Carlyle's criticism of the English social, economic, and governmental structure, he joined with one of the major streams of Victorian thought.

IV *London, Marriage, and Later Life*

For almost a year after he resigned his tutorship in the spring of 1848, Clough was at loose ends. He spent the month of May in Paris, seeing much of Ralph Waldo Emerson whom he had first come to know as the result of Emerson's acceptance of Clough's invitation to visit Oxford during the latter's last term as tutor there. The autumn was marked by two important events: the publication of Clough's *Bothie of Toper-na-Fuosich,* begun in September and published in November; and the submission of Clough's name for the principalship of University Hall, an institution founded jointly by Unitarians and Presbyterians for students at University College, London. There was apparently some hesitation on the part of the appointing board about the firmness of

Clough's stipulation that he would not superintend prayers, but the appointment was made in February, 1849, his duties to begin the following October.

January, 1849, brought the publication of *Ambarvalia*, a volume of poems Clough had written over the years at Oxford, together with a somewhat larger group of poems by his friend Thomas Burbidge. Clough and Burbidge had been trading copies of their poems for some years, but final arrangements for their publication, perhaps facilitated by the not altogether unfavorable reception awarded the *Bothie*, were not made until the autumn of 1848.

With nothing to occupy him until he took up his duties at University Hall in October, Clough left England early in April for Italy. He was thus in Rome during the short life of Mazzini's Roman Republic, which fell on June 30; but, though he sympathized with Mazzini, he seems not to have felt the need to take sides strongly or to re-examine his political and social beliefs. The outcome of his stay in Rome was, rather, the hexameter poem *Amours de Voyage* and a number of shorter poems again exploring and questioning the mysteries of the Christian religion.

Clough found the life at University Hall particularly trying. He clearly missed the more aristocratic way of life at Oxford, found it difficult to make friends, and became increasingly reserved and unsociable. He saw quite a bit of a number of important personalities—Carlyle, Walter Bagehot, Crabbe Robinson, Darwin, Palgrave—but on the whole he found his London life lonely and the post at University Hall uncongenial. Despite his opposition to the requirements of subscription to the XXXIX Articles, Clough was much more in sympathy with the atmosphere of Oxford than he could ever have been with that of London. The two letters he wrote in 1847 to the *Spectator*, taking exception (over the signature "Alpha") to F. W. Newman's lecture "On the Relation of Free Knowledge to Moral Sentiment" establish this so clearly that Clough's difficulties at London could almost have been predicted.[40]

Newman's lecture had been in effect a defense and explanation of the University of London's secular foundation, arguing that the diffusion of knowledge is in itself good, and denying that it should be "reserved in the keeping of those whose moral and spiritual culture affords some guarantee for its being well applied, and that it ought to be sedulously dealt out only to such as are willing to receive a definite moral training superadded." [41] The lecture also carried the strong implication that the restriction of knowledge to a particular group was dangerous. Clough's reply, while deprecating the subscription to the XXXIX Articles as required of tutors and fellows, insisted that the moral training undertaken at Oxford and Cambridge recognized the needs of the student more fully than the University of London system. With such a predisposition, Clough could hardly have found the atmosphere of London University comfortable. His trip to Venice in the autumn of 1850 must have been a most welcome change, though the poems which are the products of this time, especially *Dipsychus*, present ironically bitter conflicts, raising all the questions of *Ambarvalia* and extending them in new directions.

From almost the first Clough regarded his tenure of the principalship of University Hall as likely to be short, and friction developed between him and the governing council over the questions of the form religious instruction should take and over Clough's failure to attempt actively to increase the number of students. The disagreements developed to the point that Clough, who had already applied for a Chair in University College, Sydney, New South Wales, resigned in December, 1851. [42] Informed soon after that he had not been awarded the post in Sydney, Clough again found himself very much in need of a position, especially since he had already begun to consider marriage to Blanche Smith, whom he was to marry after four rather troubled years of courtship.

The agonies of this courtship having been used in Lady Chorley's biography as an index to Clough's indecisiveness, that lengthy episode deserves comment here. Since Clough left University Hall at about the time his pursuit of Blanche was becoming earnest, their courtship occurred at a most unpropitious time. Financially in no position to marry, uncertain where to turn for employment, and somewhat past the age when love generally engenders reckless optimism, Clough was naturally more hesitant in pressing his suit than most lovers. The considerable analysis of their courtship in Lady Chorley's biography does not, I think, sufficiently consider the practical difficulties of earning a livelihood which confronted Clough. Nevertheless, one must agree with her in finding Clough a most reluctant lover.

All of the more troubled letters from Clough to Blanche were understandably omitted from *Poems and Prose Remains*, and only a portion from their correspondence found its way into the Mulhauser edition. But the latter letters, supplemented by those partially reprinted by Lady Chorley, are enough to reveal the uneasiness about his relationship to Blanche. He not only writes that it would be best to call the whole thing off, but, in his attempts to express his feelings as honestly as possible, he breaks all the rules of gallantry: ". . . Do you think that though you or all womankind together cast me off that Truth would not be true, earth beautiful, the sky bright, honour honour, and work work—only a little harder. I tell you, yes; take it as you will. I ask no girl to be my friend that we may be a fond foolish couple together all in all each to the other." [43]

Worst of all perhaps, he lectures her in the same tone he had used with his little brother George: "Love is not everything, Blanche; don't believe it, nor try to make me pretend to believe it. *Service* is everything. Let us be fellow-servants. There is no joy nor happiness, nor way nor name by which men may be saved but this. . . ." [44] And: ". . . The mere man's idea of a wife as a helpmate in duty is not in my judgment an insult to womankind, though it may require modification and purification and correction. But if that were the worst sin committed against womankind, the world would be better than it is, and many women it appears to me have been misled by their aversion to this into accepting worse things. However, let us not preach. . . ." [45] This last statement sounds much like a passage Jane Austen might have put into a letter by the Mr. Collins of *Pride and Prejudice*, and one wonders where Clough's sense of humor was when he wrote that "Let us not preach."

Urged by Emerson, Clough turned toward America as a more likely place than England to earn a living. Arriving in the United States at the end of October, 1852, he found himself in very refreshing social company with Emerson, Lowell, Longfellow, and Charles Eliot Norton as his sponsors and friends. He also found himself known as the author of the *Bothie*, which seemed to have had a more successful reception among his New England friends than it had enjoyed among the English. He tutored pupils, wrote for periodicals, and thought of starting a school in America.

But the difficulty of earning enough to support a wife remained, and a strange intellectual slackness soon appears in his letters. For instance, he wearisomely reviews the advantages and disadvantages of founding a school, debating such matters as how disagreeable taking in students in his own home might be and whether or not a school could be begun in any other way. He discovered that, bracing as were the friendship and social climate, there was little more opportunity for him in America in the way of a profession than in England. The news that a position as an examiner in the Education Office was available, a post which Carlyle was largely responsible for finding him, caused a period of unhappy indecision. The choice was in effect made for him by his wife-to-be, and he returned to England in July, 1853, and was married on June 12, 1854.

From this point on Clough's life seems to have flowed evenly along. He apparently did not dislike the work connected with the examinership, despite its monotony; and there is every evidence that he found contentment in the roles of husband and father. He regarded the chance to render services to Florence Nightingale, his wife's cousin, a pleasurable duty. These services extended far beyond the tying up of brown-paper parcels scornfully referred to by Lytton Strachey, including as they did considerable editorial work of a kind for which Clough was well fitted. On the other hand, he found little time for poetry. He did revise the *Bothie* and reworked *Amours de Voyage* before allowing Lowell to publish it in the *Atlantic Monthly* from March to May, 1858. Other time went to continuing the revision of an edition of Plutarch which he had begun before returning to England (published 1859) and translating passages of Homer for his own pleasure.

In December, 1859, Clough was stricken with scarlatina, which weakened his health to such an extent that he never fully recovered. After travelling about England in the attempt to recoup his strength, he found it necessary to apply for additional leave from the Education Office. His health seeming to improve over the winter, he travelled to Greece and back and thence to France and Italy, hoping always for a complete recuperation; but his condition worsened in Italy. He died in Florence on November 13, 1861, and is buried in the Protestant Cemetery there.

It has been pointed out that all of Clough's longer, more ambitious poems were written during vacation travels. He seemed to require both leisure and the stimulation of travel to compose more than a brief poem. Despite his illness, he began his first new long poem in many years during the travels of his last two years. The result was the unfinished *Mari Magno,* a series somewhat after the manner of Chaucer's *Canterbury Tales.*

V *Clough as a Representative Figure*

The custom of contrasting Clough's questionings in the 1840's with the affirmations of Matthew Arnold in the 1860's and 1870's has made Clough seem more wayward and eccentric than he was. In writing of his personal complexities, Clough was expressing the conscientious revaluation of older beliefs which occupied many of the men of his university generation. Tom Arnold's distress at the mood and temper of the age has already been mentioned. Like Clough, he wished to discover for himself a sure ground for religious faith and to find a vocation untainted by selfishness and dishonesty; and, also like Clough, he was earnest enough about these things to be prepared to make large sacrifices. His faith in the virtue of hard work led him to New Zealand as a farmer; when practical difficulties brought this plan to an end, he hoped, again like Clough, to become a part of a more liberal and at the same time more serious educational system than existed at the two great English universities.

When it looked as if Arnold might be given the principalship of the proposed Nelson College in New Zealand, he wrote to Clough expressing his hope that Clough and Shairp might come out and join him in "a glorious onslaught on the great kingdom of darkness. . . ." [46] A few months later he wrote: "Here where we could work with a free activity, we might lay the foundations deep and wide, of an institution, which like Iona in the middle ages, might one day spread the light of Religion and Letters over these barbarous colonies and throughout the great archipelago of the Pacific, where hitherto only the white man's avarice or lust or his imbecile Theology have penetrated." [47]

Through their sense of shared idealism, Clough and Tom Arnold were probably much more closely linked than Clough and Matthew Arnold. The following letter from Tom Arnold to Clough, which in print perhaps carries a ring of pious egotism, represents what nevertheless was a totally sincere and, within its context, natural expression of both men's sense of duty:

How little do I know of all that that capacious head of yours is scheming and imagining; yet how certain I feel, that whatever be the

particular objects of its activity, truth is ever its pole-star, and moral
nobleness its guide. And, I too, dear soul-friend, am less changed than
you might imagine. Some intellectual weapons, which in old days, I
may have essayed to wield with what little strength I had, may be
now rusted for lack of use; that is alas! only too possible for a man
situated as I am, with so few to exchange thoughts with; but the great
hope within—the grand effort of the will—the great beacon lights of
life—remain what they were, and point in the same direction as of
old.[48]

Tom Arnold's quest for a resolution of his religious questioning
led him to the Catholic Church, which he joined in 1856. His desire to find a position in the world from which he could work
effectively for his ideals lay behind his decision to accept an appointment at the Catholic University of Dublin to which Newman had been appointed rector. He later followed Newman to the
Birmingham Oratory school, broke for a time with Catholicism,
rejoined that church, and finally settled at the Royal University of
Ireland in Dublin. His life would seem to have been devoted to
the uncompromising pursuit of high ideals, following his scruples
wherever they led; but his moral rigor left him always unsatisfied.
In his autobiographical *Passages in a Wandering Life*, he writes,
in Thomas Seccombe's words, "of a life which he laments, with
needless bitterness, that the greater part had been 'restless and
unprofitable.' " [49]

The combination of conscientiousness and skepticism represented by Clough and Tom Arnold was not limited to those who
had experienced the direct influence of Dr. Arnold. J. A. Froude,
Clough's friend and almost exact contemporary, resigned his fellowship at Exeter College on the ground of religious reservations.
Though his accuracy as a historian was under heavy fire in his
own time and remains moot, he endeavored to examine both contemporary and historical problems with painstaking care. The result of his analysis of the religious doubts of his own generation
was the novel *The Nemesis of Faith* which Clough described in a
letter to Edward Hawkins as presenting "a good deal" of the religious difficulties encountered by "the young world in general." [50]

Clough must have found the opinions expressed in the book
extremely congenial. The distaste of the protagonist, Sutherland,
for the necessary sophistries of the various professions anticipates
Dipsychus's similar feelings, and his preference for the solid doc-

trines of Bishops Butler and Berkeley anticipate points Clough was to make in his University of London lectures. Most important, Sutherland debates the conflicting claims of action and speculation just as do Clough's characters. Both Froude and Clough were under the influence of Carlyle; but, though Froude was later to become a true disciple, both must at this time have been feeling somewhat betrayed. Sutherland is portrayed as finding Carlyle insufficient—"Carlyle only raises questions he cannot answer, and seems best contented if he can make the rest of us as discontented as himself" [51]—which sounds very much like Clough's famous remark to Emerson that "Carlyle has led us all out into the desert, and he has left us there." [52] But, like Clough, Froude was, as his preface to the second edition shows, clinging to the doctrine of action as a talisman to break the circle of barren speculation—"It is as idle for the mind to hope to speculate clear of doubt in the closet, as for the body to be physicked out of sickness kept lying on a sofa. Employment is for one what exercise is for the other." [53]

It is, I think, important to an understanding of Clough to recall the careers of such men as Thomas Arnold and Froude. Not a few members of his university generation, including some of his closest friends, found themselves faced with painful intellectual questions; their resolutions of them involved considerable personal sacrifice.

CHAPTER 2

Reaction to Oxford: The Bothie

C LOUGH'S first significant published poem was *The Bothie of Toper-na-Fuosich*, a lengthy hexameter narrative of the adventures of a long-vacation reading party to the Highlands and the successive romances and resulting marriage of one of the party, Philip Hewson. The surprise occasioned by the publication of the idyllic *Bothie* at a time when all Clough's friends were expecting some kind of serious poetic defense of his decision to leave Oxford has been widely remarked. However, the poem was, and is, bound to be a surprise to any reader coming to it for the first time, regardless of his preconceptions. Part of the surprise lies in the contrast between the poem's homely content and its bizarre title, taken from the Gaelic name of a Highland forester's hut, or "bothie." When the original Gaelic form Toper-na-Fuosich was found to have indelicate connotations, Clough modified it to the meaningless Tober-na-Vuolich.[1]

The outlandish title is matched by Clough's use of what must remain in English poetry an outlandish meter, and by the curious mixture of seemingly incompatible ingredients. The description of an Oxford reading party becomes lost in an idyllic handling of a love affair; a strong matter-of-factness of statement exists in conflict with the series of most unlikely coincidences that lead Philip to Elspie; a style which Matthew Arnold praised for its closeness to the Homeric becomes at times clearly a parody of the epic; and a phrasing which is sometimes so ungainly as to suggest a schoolboy's burlesque of Classical rhetorical devices veers at other times toward an almost cloyingly sentimental debate over the role of women, a debate which extends itself at times into the whole area of social and economic justice.

I *The Meter*

One is almost obliged, because of their strangeness, to begin
with a discussion of Clough's hexameters, the place of which in
English poetry is thorny indeed. Southey initiated the nineteenth-
century interest in the form with *The Vision of Judgment,* and a
number of experiments, including translations of the *Iliad,* were
made in hexameters in succeeding decades. Longfellow's *Evange-
line* of 1847 won for the form considerably more approval than it
has generally enjoyed, but at the same time aroused considerable
learned controversy over the propriety of the meter.

Despite Longfellow's apparent success, the form has never been
domesticated; when Clough chose to follow him in making use of
the hexameter, he doomed his poem to a place in the never-
concluded debate over the hexameter's suitability in English. At
least two schools flatly deny its appropriateness on the grounds
either that there can be no *good* English hexameter or that it is
impossible to write English hexameter at all. Critical discussion of
the hexameter is complicated by the controversy between those
who think the English treatment should reproduce as far as possible the effect of the Classical meter and those who feel that its
success should be judged quite apart from such expectations. And,
finally, there arise such questions as whether the English hexameter should be based on accentual or quantitative values (or some
combination of the two); and whether, if the latter, normal pro-
nunciation or a special theory of syllabic values should govern.

It is perhaps enough to say of Clough's theory that, like Longfellow and Southey, he chose the accentual basis, using the Classical dactyl and spondee; but he gave himself considerable freedom
in handling the form, as is evidenced by his note on the back of
the title page: "The reader is warned to expect every kind of ir-
regularity in these modern hexameters: spondaic lines, so called,
are almost the rule; and a word will often require to be trans-
posed by the voice from the end of one line to the beginning of
the next."

Critics have disagreed widely about the success of Clough's approach. George Saintsbury pronounced his hexameters to be intolerable and cited him as a prime example of what the poet should
avoid.[2] C. H. Herford, speaking of both the *Bothie* and *Amours*

de Voyage, found that Clough may "claim to have written three
or four of the finest English hexameters; but it is almost as certain
that he has to answer for a hundred or more of the worst." [3] On
the other hand, Robert Graves, not a fancier of the meter, cited
Clough's as a most enjoyable exception to the overall failure of the
English hexameter.[4] In Matthew Arnold's well-known reference
to the *Bothie* in his lectures *On Translating Homer,* Clough's handling of the form was judged, although rough and comically grotesque, more like the *Iliad* "than any other English poem which I
can call to mind . . . in the rapidity of its movement, and the
plainness and directness of its style." [5]

And Charles Kingsley, whose own hexameters in *Andromeda*
Saintsbury thought excellent (while arguing that their excellence
is derived precisely from the fact that Kingsley employs a line
which is not a hexameter at all but a "five-foot anapaestic with
anacrusis [odd syllable at the beginning] and hypercatalexis
[ditto at the end]"),[6] pronounced the *Bothie* to contain "some of
the most perfect hexameters, in our humble opinion, which we
have yet seen in the English language. When the author has given
himself fair play, he has shown a complete mastery over the metre
and a faculty . . . of Anglicizing the metre, of harmonizing, not
English to it, but it to English." [7]

In any case, for readers coming to the *Bothie* for the first time,
Clough's lines are likely to appear to fall awkwardly between two
stools. Read as poetry, they may well seem to defy attempts to
read them rhythmically, both because the extra foot seems super-
fluous and because the uncertainty of scansion allows the dactyls
to break down into anapaests. Clough himself recognized the
difficulties encountered by the reader of English hexameters. The
"uncle" of the Prologue to *Dipsychus* complains of his earlier
verse that "Nothing is more disagreeable than to say a line over
two, or, it may be, three or four times, and at last not be sure that
there are not three or four ways of reading, each as good and as
much intended as another." Similarly, in one of his discussions of
the problem of translation, Clough finds Homer and Virgil's verse
"totally unlike those lengthy, straggling, irregular, uncertain slips
of *prose measurée* which we find it so hard to measure, so easy to
read in half-a-dozen ways, without any assurance of the right
one. . . ." [8] The "uncle" also demurs about Clough's earlier

"hurry-scurry anapaests," a phrase which may well indicate that Clough was quite aware of the tendency of the English hexameter to break down into anapaestic feet.

On the other hand, the reader who, content to lose the meter, tries to read the *Bothie* as prose finds this equally impossible. The inversions, the repetitions of opening phrases for two and sometimes three lines (a favorite device of Clough's and one licensed by Classical poets), the continual encounter with lines and parts of lines which do scan easily and naturally, as well as the printing of the work as a poem, constantly lead the reader into new attempts to find and to feel the prosodic structure. The result of perseverance is, hopefully, the accommodation of the reader's ear to the hexameter proper. Perhaps the best way of accustoming oneself to the form is to forget all the theories about it, taking care only that one reads each line with the first stress on the first syllable.[9]

Readers understandably vary in their response to Clough's intentional roughness of meter and awkwardness of phrase. The many lines which simply will not scan—and even those who most defend the hexameter and Clough's use of it admit that there are many such—tend to be extremely annoying. Moreover, the contrast between the lyrical tone of much of the latter portion of the poem, especially the last two sections, and the thorniness introduced into passages of essentially "correct" hexameters by needless inversions and awkward, densely punctuated syntactical constructions makes one especially regret the rough passages.

The following passage, though it has been praised for its metrical correctness,[10] is undeniably awkward.

> How the old knightly religion, the chivalry semi-quixotic
> Stirs in the veins of a man at seeing some delicate woman
> Serving him, toiling—for him, and the world; some tenderest
>   girl, now
> Over-weighted, expectant, of him, is it? who shall, if only
> Duly her burden be lightened, not wholly removed from her,
>   mind you,
> Lightened if but by the love, the devotion man only can
>   offer,
> Grand on her pedestal rise as urn-bearing statue of Hellas;—
>   (124)

One may compare the cited passage with Clough's hexameters at
their lyrical best:

> It was on Saturday eve, in the gorgeous bright October,
> Then when brackens are changed, and heather blooms are
>   faded,
> And amid russet of heather and fern green trees are bonnie;
> Alders are green, and oaks; the rowan scarlet and yellow;
> One great glory of broad gold pieces appears the aspen,
> And the jewels of gold that were hung in the hair of the
>   birch-tree,
> Pendulous, here and there, her coronet, necklace, and ear-
>   rings,
> Cover her now, o'er and o'er; she is weary and scatters them
>   from her.
>
> (164)

Moreover, Clough's gentle mockery of the Classics at times adds
as much awkwardness as humor. The "grotesque" diction and
"odd epithets," as in the "grave man nicknamed Adam," were de-
fended by Arnold as natural in a "serio-comic" poem; but these
essentially mock-heroic phrasings, like Clough's humorous exploi-
tation of other Classical rhetorical devices, become at times
wearying. For instance, the frequent repetition of lines and
phrases, a parody of a Classical rhetorical figure more often than
an esthetic embellishment, is a humorous device which grows
stale after the first section of the *Bothie*.

There remains the question of just what effect Clough wished to
achieve by his hexameters. It has been held that they are appropriate to the tone of light humor which most readers find in the
poem, but it has also been argued that the hexameters are appropriate to a simple dignity much like that in Goethe's *Hermann
and Dorothea*. Interestingly, the anonymous author of the "Dialogue on English Hexameters" published in the December, 1847,
number of *Fraser's Magazine* argued that the Goethe poem could
only be translated into English in hexameters; in March, 1849,
after the publication of the *Bothie*, the same writer pointed out in
a second "dialogue" that Clough's hexameters did indeed produce
an effect equivalent to that of *Hermann and Dorothea*.[11]

II *The Story and Its Significance*

The substance of the poem is at least as incongruous as the
form. In the opening sections Clough is obviously enjoying describing an Oxford reading party, part of the enjoyment coming
from his private memories of such parties in which he has partici-
pated and part from a mock-heroic treatment of the members of
the party. Tags are attached to their names in diminutive echo of
the Homeric style, "cigar-loving Lindsay" replacing "red-haired
Menelaus" and "Arthur, the glory of Headers" replacing "Diome-
des, tamer of horses." Trivial incidents are reported as worthy of
inclusion in an epic: "Be it recorded in song who was first, who
last, in dressing." The first Homeric simile occurs as early as line
ninety; and, once the mock-heroic parallel has been set going, the
dinner, closed by Philip's speech in Section I, faintly recalls
Homer's feasts and hero's speeches.

In Section II arises the discussion of the comparative charms of
the upper-class women who are brought up as in a hothouse
versus those of "the out-of-door beauties;/Meadow and woodland
sweets" who gain, according to Philip, an added charm from the
grace with which their beauty becomes the humble domestic
tasks they perform. Clough, who treats the debate with high good
humor, gives Arthur and Hobbes the opportunity to compare
laughingly Philip's championship of the woman "Bending with
three-pronged fork in a garden uprooting potatoes" to Pugin's
championship of Gothic architecture. But Clough's endlessly
speculative tendency has, by the end of the section, already
moved to a broader level of questioning; and he begins to explore
the justice of the class system. Adam the tutor argues that one
should do one's duty in one's station, to which Philip replies

> *Doing our duty in that state of life to which God has called
>   us,*
> Seems to me always to mean, when the little rich boys say it,
> Standing in velvet frock by mama's brocaded flounces,
>
> . . . .
> Seems to me always to mean, Eat, drink, and never mind
>   others.

(128)

The background set, Philip is allowed to become successively enamored with three women. The first is Katie, the farmer's daughter, who enchants Philip as much by going "through beating rain to the peat-stack" as by her beauty; the second is the Lady Maria, who for a moment reverses all his theories and leads him to exclaim "Perish the poor and the weary! what can they better than perish,/Perish in labour for her, who is worth the destruction of empires?" (150). The third is Elspie, who lives at the Bothie (or hut) of Toper-na-Fuosich.

Though Elspie's father now lives as a frugal highland farmer, Clough gives to the daughter, as well as to her sister and father, a kind of natural gentility which makes it possible for her to represent a balance between Katie and the Lady Maria. The solution, the product of unchecked sentimental idealism, is contrived so as to allow Philip to marry a girl who refuses to live a life so useless as that of a "Lady" but who possesses graces not necessarily, or even generally, learned while digging potatoes or carrying peats. The Tutor, it is clear, feels that Philip's choice has been made in accordance with his own advice to choose the "Good" above the attractive; but why Katie, for instance, does not represent the "Good" is not made entirely clear, unless it is that she has the good sense not to allow Philip's fickleness to break her heart.

In some ways the whole poem represents a struggle between Clough's idealism, realism, and social conscience. The problems of the social conscience are finally side-stepped by the romantic conclusion of the poem, even as Philip's scruples disappear in his love for Elspie:

> So that the whole great wicked artificial civilised fabric—
> All its unfinished houses, lots for sale, and railway out-
> works—
> Seems reaccepted, resumed to Primal Nature and Beauty:—
> —Such—in me, and to me, and on me the love of Elspie!
> (172)

Clough's ironic realism has its play especially in the outlook of Hobbes, whose letter to Philip at the end of Section V goes well beyond Victorian propriety (especially in the double entendre of the last lines quoted below) as he continues his satire of Philip's theory of women:

Every Woman is, or ought to be, a Cathedral,
. . . .
Built by that only law, that Use be suggester of Beauty,
Nothing concealed that is done, but all things done to adorn-
    ment,
Meanest utilities seized as occasion to grace and embellish.—

Hobbes then asks the destructively realistic question:

She that is handy is handsome, good dairy-maids must be
    good-looking,
If but the butter be nice, the tournor of the elbow is shapely,
If the cream-cheeses be white, far whiter the hands that
    made them,
If—but alas, is it true?

                                        (151–52)

But, after all, Clough's idealism and romanticism are what win
through in the *Bothie,* and to these qualities the seventh and
eighth sections are devoted: Elspie's blushing confession in the
dusk, her feeling of an inferiority to Philip, her well-known comparison of herself to a "poor, slender burnie" and of Philip to the
sea, "Forcing its great strong tide into every nook and inlet,"
Philip's belief that women intuitively "know all beforehand" and
thus do not need to read books—all of these are expressions of
Clough's idealism about women, love, and life. The fact that he
was willing to sink his speculations about the role of women and
the justice of the social structure in a romantic conclusion is as
good evidence as one could have of Clough's high spirits and
sense of relief at leaving Oxford; and the event itself is perhaps a
foreshadowing of the ascendancy of the more comfortable attitude toward the world that marriage would later bring about.

It is significant that Philip is sent off to a happy life farming in
New Zealand, a choice probably suggested by that of Tom Arnold, but one which must have also symbolically reflected
Clough's feeling of entering a new and more vital world when he
left Oxford. The larger questions of the rightness of each man's
role in life and of the possibility of discovering with certainty his
duties are also left unresolved. These questions are again discussed inconclusively in the last section in which Adam sums up
his beliefs under the figure of a battle:

> There is a great Field-Marshal, my friend, who arrays our
>   battalions;
> Let us to Providence trust, and abide and work in our
>   stations.

Philip questions the significance of the metaphor:

> I am sorry to say your Providence puzzles me sadly;
> Children of Circumstance are we to be? you answer, On no
>   wise!
> Where does Circumstance end, and Providence where be-
>   gins it?
> What are we to resist, and what are we to be friends with?
> If there is battle, 'tis battle by night: I stand in the darkness,
> Here in the mêlée of men, Ionian and Dorian on both sides,
> Signal and password known; which is friend and which is
>   foeman?

Yet Philip is willing to let the question drop after merely stating
his caveat: "Though I mistrust the Field-Marshal, I bow to the
duty of order" (170).

The hopeful tone on which the poem ends is not created only
by the speeches of the two lovers; the most structurally happy portion of the poem is the closing passage of the last section. After a gesture toward the mock-heroic in the form of a catalogue of wedding gifts, Hobbes's final letter, picking up the allusions which have been made to the ideal woman and to Elspie as
like Jacob's Rachel, comments upon the story of Jacob, Leah, and
Rachel as an allegory of marriage:

> For this Rachel-and-Leah is marriage, and Laban their father
> Circumstance, chance, the world, our uncle and hard task-
>   master.
> Rachel we found as we fled from the daughters of Heth by
>   the desert;
> Rachel we met at the well; we came, we saw, we kissed her;
> Rachel we serve-for, long years,—that seem as a few days
>   only,
> E'en for the love we have to her,—and win her at last of
>   Laban.
> Is it not Rachel we take in our joy from the hand of the
>   father?

Is it not Rachel we lead in the mystical veil from the altar?
Rachel we dream-of at night: in the morning, behold, it is
    Leah.
'Nay, it is custom,' saith Laban, the Leah indeed is the elder.
Happy and wise who consents to redouble his service to
    Laban,
So, fulfilling her week, he may add to the elder the younger,
Not repudiates Leah, but wins the Rachel unto her!

                                                    (174)

After all, marriage and love, like all of life, are compounds of
the heavenly and the earthy; that by hard labor rendered to "Circumstance, chance, the world, our uncle and hard taskmaster"
the balance is tipped toward the ideal is one of the answers to the
puzzle of life to which Clough kept returning. Here it is expressed
more happily, with less residue of inartistic abstraction, than usual
in Clough's poetry. The *Bothie* reveals much about Clough's state
of mind at this time and to some extent anticipates his later development. Significantly, in the first place, religious questions find
hardly a place in the poem. It is true that, when Philip's question
about the justice of the social classes leads to a consideration of
the amount of trust to be placed in Providence, Clough is only one
step away from raising all the questions of *Ambarvalia;* he would
have done so if the meaning of "Providence" had been examined
more closely. (It would seem that Philip's mind here is reflecting
Clough's own tendency to pursue all things to first principles and
thus to question that of man's relationship to God.) But this step
is avoided, and the poem ends on a bright note.

That the buoyancy of the poem is a result of Clough's sense of
relief at leaving Oxford can hardly be doubted (although there
have been those who questioned the degree of that relief),[12] but
it seems unlikely that that tone could have been sustained through
the poem had Clough still been haunted by religious doubts. He
was able to exclude the subject from the *Bothie* because he felt it
had been largely solved, and this view was not altogether an illusion. The poems of *Ambarvalia*, though not couched in theological
terms, are an expression of Clough's doubts about the adequacy of
traditional Anglican doctrine. With his rejection of the orthodoxy
of the XXXIX Articles, Clough had indeed solved one problem;
his later religious poems turn to other kinds of questions.

Second, the problems which are treated in the *Bothie* are in a sense practical: how to choose a wife and to what extent to oppose the established order. The spirit in which the answers are given is, as has been pointed out again and again, Carlylean. Clough is, for the moment, ready to affirm the "everlasting Yea," though he will find that in practice this affirmation is difficult.

The interest in love and marriage is natural to one of Clough's age, and the speculative approach is appropriate for one of his cast of mind; but a number of commentators have gone further. In a delightful essay Maurice Hewlett finds the joyousness of the poem and its treatment of love natural only to one who is in love. To Hewlett, the poem is the product of Carlyle's appeal to the intellect combined with a love affair's appeal to the emotions.[13] Lady Chorley has pointed out a passage in a letter of 1846 from Clough to his sister Anne which seems to indicate that Clough was contemplating marriage; she also finds evidence of the collapse of Clough's hopes in several poems written at the time.[14] The likelihood that there was a Marguerite in Clough's life as well as in Arnold's has also been argued by A. M. Turner; and Goldie Levy reminds one that Thackeray reported after meeting Clough in 1848 that "he has evidently been crossed in love." [15]

The matter remains obscure and conjectural, however; no clues have so far been discovered as to who the woman in question might have been. (From subsequent letters and poems, one feels that what Clough needed was just the Elspie who, with a single glance, could make up a man's mind for him without his realizing it.) Clough, further, is willing to grant love, at least in Philip, its full power as expressed by Carlyle: "If in youth . . . the Universe is majestically unveiling, and everywhere Heaven revealing itself on Earth, nowhere to the Young Man does this Heaven on Earth so immediately reveal itself as in the Young Maiden." [16]

The question of how to find one's proper place in, and relation to, the social order, though, as has been seen, not explicitly resolved, is implicitly answered by Philip's going to New Zealand. The figure of Philip is probably derived from Clough's own sanguine hopes and from his admiration for Tom Arnold. We know that emigrating appealed to Clough at one time, and in the *Bothie* he is quite likely expressing his sympathy with Arnold's decision to go to New Zealand. Hard practical work (Thomas Arnold's original intention was to settle as a farmer) should be the man's part (thus also the appreciative treatment of David Mackaye, "How on his pittance of soil he lived, and raised potatoes,/Barley, and oats, in the bothie where lived his father before him") to which the woman's useful lighter toil was the fit complement. Clough is affirming the doctrine of *Past and Present:* "work is alone noble."

But Philip's departure for New Zealand is not only an expression of appreciation for Tom's decision, it is also a symbol for Clough's own decision to leave Oxford and engage in practical activity in the great world. The two acts were closely linked in Clough's mind; a letter to Tom in New Zealand avers: "but for thy departure I should perhaps be still lingering undecided in the courts of conformity." [17] J. I. Osborne is perhaps overstating the situation when he says that to Clough, during his last years as a tutor at Oxford, "Oxford was the actual, soiled, everyday thing; human life outside the walls, the divine mystery." [18] But it is true enough that Clough came to feel that the secret of life was not to be found at Oxford but in the world outside. Adam, the tutor, for all the wisdom and goodness to which Clough pays homage, is a bit priggish, a bit comical in his awkwardness in the world outside Oxford. One might say that in some respects Adam represents the too-cloistered Clough of the past and Philip the active man Clough desired to become in the future. Again one thinks of Carlyle: "The end of Man is an Action, and not a Thought."

One can hardly leave the *Bothie* without pointing out its interest as an index of the literary taste of the time, especially of the average Oxford don. It is amusing, but very revealing of the Oxford atmosphere, to note that Clough reported the *Bothie* was regarded as "indecent and profane, immoral and (!) Communistic" and that Hawkins, the Provost of Oriel, took exception to some parts as "rather indelicate." [19] R. W. Church also lamented the existence of some "coarse" lines in the *Bothie.* Clough himself seems to have felt that some of the phrasing in the poem was too exuberant; in the revision to which he submitted the poem in 1859 and 1860, he not only cut down some of the longer speeches and made minor stylistic alterations but removed, apparently as indelicate, lines as inoffensive to the modern eyes as "You will have seen yourself the danger of pantry-flirtation." [20] It is equally noteworthy that its foremost public defender, Charles Kingsley, praised it not so much for its verve and humor as for the purpose he found stated there: *"To make people do their duty in that state of life to which God has called them."* [21]

CHAPTER 3

A Mind in Tension: Ambarvalia

A mbarvalia: Poems by Thomas Burbidge and Arthur Hugh
Clough was published in January, 1849, two months after the
Bothie. As the product of his years of self-questioning at Oxford,
Clough's contributions to the volume, all probably in their final
state before the writing of the *Bothie*, reveal many issues in the
conflict which had come to a temporary resolution at the time of
his resignation from Oxford. Though not a defense of his resignation or a manifesto, the poems reveal the precise nature of the
radical uncertainties with which Clough was struggling and the
entire conscientiousness with which he attempted to face every
question; thus, in a sense, they provide that explanation which his
friends had expected of the *Bothie*. The reaction of most of his
friends does not, however, indicate that they were able either to
enter sympathetically into Clough's perplexities or to see for what
purpose he was using his poetry. "When soft September brings
again" and "Light Words," both representing moods and subjects
peripheral to the volume, were singled out for the greatest
amount of praise in their congratulatory letters.

The title of the volume is taken from the ancient Roman festival
at which animals were sacrificed to insure the fertility of the fields.
The reasons behind the choice of the title must remain conjectural; it has little apparent relevance to the poems included by
either Clough or Burbidge. To those familiar with Clough's life
and poetry, however, the title can perhaps be recognized as having a certain significance beyond whatever Clough intended; his
portion of the volume, for the most part, represents the sacrifice of
an enormous amount of painful energy in the attempt to propiti-
ate the spirit, or demon, of absolute intellectual honesty which
Clough so honored.

The opening poem of the volume, for which Clough later suggested the title "The Questioning Spirit," introduces in its first stanza an emblem of Clough's intellectual life:

> The human spirits saw I on a day,
> Sitting and looking each a different way;
> And hardly tasking, subtly questioning,
> Another spirit went around the ring
> To each and each: and as he ceased his say,
> Each after each, I heard them singly sing,
> Some querulously high, some softly, sadly low,
> We know not,—what avails to know?
> We know not, wherefore need we know?
> This answer gave they still unto his suing,
> We know not, let us do as we are doing.

That each man indeed pursues his own goals while unwilling to entertain and unable to answer fundamental questions of what or how or why, represents the human condition as many besides Clough have seen it. But this vision, from which many another thinker has pushed forward to found a system satisfactory at least to himself in giving the answers to how or why, Clough found enormous difficulty in transcending. This particular poem comes to a resolution in approval for the seventh spirit's devotion to a duty the larger meaning of which he cannot know. It is, however, just here that Clough in other poems confesses himself balked: how can one know what is duty when one is in "true ignorance" of all else? Furthermore, the questioning spirit itself, clearly intended in this poem to present the doing of one's duty as the best guide amid human ignorance, is later seen ambivalently; perhaps that spirit tempts to destruction.

Clough's contributions to *Ambarvalia* answer variously the problems raised by such questioning. Some, like the "Commemorative Sonnets," "Alcaics" and "When soft September," seem practice exercises; but most strike one not so much as either carefully finished esthetic objects or powerfully stated formulations of the poet's beliefs as so many instances of the trying-out of ideas in poetic form. The inconsistency of the lines of argument in these poems demonstrates the seriousness and the difficulty of the problems raised. This use of poetry as a medium for the expression of problems makes Clough a philosophic poet in an almost unique sense.

In one of his undergraduate essays Clough distinguished satire
from "genuine Poetry," describing the latter as "careless of the
present" and as "impatient in its love for the end of the anxieties
and struggles of the pursuit." [1] Clough's own employment of poetry as a means of speculation is, like satire, too concerned with
present problems, with discords and struggles, to achieve the finished surface and integrated view one associates with "genuine
Poetry" or, that is, poetry which takes beauty as its object.

The attempts which have been made to argue that Clough
either was, or should have been, primarily a satirist, are to some
extent based on a partial recognition of this point. Finding considerable portions of his work satirical, certain critics have tended to
explain as in some way satiric the other portions which obviously
do not aim at poetic beauty; they fail to recognize that what
Clough aimed at in these poems was neither the lyric nor the satiric. This is not to say that Clough was not at times very witty
and at other moments quite the opposite of prudish in his irony. A
collection of all those passages excised, as the phrase is, "pro
pudore," either by the poet himself or his wife in her capacity as
editor, would prove a valuable corrective to the usual view of
Clough as a prime representative of inhibited Victorianism. [2]

I   Truth and Duty

The human problems considered in *Ambarvalia* are of the
broadest import. There is, first, a whole array of attitudes toward
the vexed question of duty. The well-known "Qui Laborat, Orat,"
argues that life properly lived and work properly done are in
themselves a perpetual prayer; God is known aright in "the hours
of mortal moral strife" and not presumably by abstract medita-
tion. Work is thus prayer, worship, and the means of achieving
"The beatific supersensual sight."

Thomas Arnold has referred the genesis of this poem to an evening's discussion of the dangers of vocal prayers, but it almost
surely owes as much to Carlyle as to that conversation. "Admi-
rable was that of the old Monks, '*Laborare est Orare*,' work is
worship," is the burden of Chapter XII of *Past and Present*. [3] But
we know from other poems of *Ambarvalia* that the Carlylean faith
is not sufficient for Clough; in the background lies the question:
"what *is* the work which is worthy?"

The pitfalls of blindly following what seems to be duty are pre-

sented in a pair of poems. That which begins "Thought may well
be ever ranging" warns of the danger of mistaking duty for love—

> Men and maidens, see you mind it;
> Show of love, where'er you find it,
> Look if duty lurk behind it!
> Duty-fancies, urging on
> Whither love had never gone!

The poem beginning "Duty—that's to say complying" looks forward to *Dipsychus* in its irony and prosody. Duty, it argues, can
be simply compliance with social norms, or worse, the excuse for
sacrificing "all that's truest, noblest, best" in a refusal to follow the
soul in its questing and guessing. The fear of acquiescing in a
partial truth, of compromising, and of accepting duties ready-
made appears also in "Come back again my olden heart" which
prefers a courageous refusal to make questionable affirmations to
the attitude which proudly wills to "climb and soar aloft" above
doubts and fears.

One begins to see running through all these poems two patterns
of thought which go far to explain what is too easily interpreted
as mere indecisiveness and fruitless questioning. The first is a fear
of making irrevocable decisions—not only decisions which might
lead to practical tragedies, as in the possibility of confusing love
and duty, but also decisions which might begin to corrupt the
freedom and purity of the mind. "Skepticism is the chastity of the
mind" says Santayana, and Clough seems to have been one who
would take this statement in an almost literal sense. Premature
decisions and unconscious compromises are dangerous not only
because they preclude other possible views and beliefs, but because, in a sense which can be expressed only metaphorically,
they clutter, sully, and finally destroy the temple of the mind in
which Clough hopes some day a revelation will occur. This attitude is discoverable in a letter dating from 1836, when Clough
was in the fifth form at Rugby, in which he speaks of feeling "triumphant" in knowing that his heart "was sanctified for a temple
of God's spirit." [4] However unnaturally pious the sentiment may
seem in a boy of seventeen, such phrases in Clough's letters were
not merely conventional pieties but represented the basis of his
later attitude toward the world.

The poetic cry "Come back again, my olden heart!" questions whether the "heavenly light" which reveals "the truly right" can still be expected to reveal itself once he has dismissed the doubting heart which kept the world and compromise at bay. But, if the mind preserves itself uncluttered and inviolate, then—and this is a position to which Clough tenaciously holds at this time—the light, the revelation, and the vision will appear. Viewed in this way, "Qui Laborat, Orat" expresses the hope that some form of direct knowledge of God will be granted to one who expresses his devotion through work, and thus avoids speculation about or egoistic claims on the deity.

The clearest statement of this view is perhaps in the brief poem beginning "Away, haunt not thou me." Vain philosophy, which offers only "to perplex the head,/and leave the spirit dead," is contrasted with the Wisdom and Power "welling, bubbling forth, unseen, incessantly." The last four lines are probably more often quoted than fully understood within the context of Clough's thought:

> Why labour at the dull mechanic oar,
> When the fresh breeze is blowing,
> And the strong current flowing,
> Right onward to the Eternal Shore?

The poem dismisses mechanic philosophy to wait on direct inspiration and revelation—but, despite the cheering tone, the bulk of Clough's treatments assume that the wait may be a long and dreary one. For all his evocation of "secret treasure-depths below,/Fed by the skiey shower,/And clouds that sink and rest on hill-tops high," he cannot share the faiths held by the Romantic poets who might well have written those lines.

Clough was a great admirer of Wordsworth, not only in his Rugby days but at Oxford.[5] One of his most ambitious essays at Rugby was in that poet's praise, and J. C. Shairp records Clough's speaking against the proposition "that Tennyson was a greater poet than Wordsworth" at the Decade.[6] But for this very reason, nothing shows the doubting temper of Clough's mind better than comparison with the younger Wordsworth. For the Romantic poet, the glimpses of Eternity were to be encountered on all sides, in the meanest flower that blows as well as in the sublimity of the Alps. But, for Clough, the times when "Unsummoned powers the blinding film shall part,/And scarce by happy tears made dim, the eyes/in recognition start" are extremely rare, and more anticipated than experienced. Clough seems to have had an ironic sense of this difference, for when he most closely and intentionally echoes Wordsworth, the echo becomes mocking:

> Here am I yet, another twelvemonth spent,
> One-third departed of the mortal span,
> Carrying on the child into the man,
> Nothing into reality
> . . . .
> So was it from the first, so is it yet;
> Yes, the first kiss that by these lips was set
> On any human lips, methinks was sin—

The child may well be father of the man, but this thought is hardly comforting to one unable to look back upon a childhood trailing any discernible clouds of glory. Indeed, the poem from which the above lines are taken is one of a series bearing the title "Blank Misgivings of a Creature moving about in Worlds not realized"—a phrase taken from Wordsworth's "Ode: Intimations of Immortality," where it is charged with much more hopeful connotations than it conveys standing alone as Clough's title. Similarly, the last section of "When panting sighs the bosom fill," which contains such Wordsworthian lines as "A glory on the vision lay;/A light of more than mortal day/About it played, upon it rested," is introduced by a mockingly phrased answer to the question of whether it is true love that is felt: "I cannot say—the things are good:/Bread is it, if not angel's food;/But Love? Alas! I cannot say; . . ." And indeed whether a glory lay on the vision or not, Clough is unsure whether its source is not "Fancy's brook, or [sexual] Passion's river."

Despite his admiration, the mature Clough was not prepared to admit that Wordsworth's affirmations were based on entirely solid ground; and his criticism in his lectures at the University of London reflects his own fears of premature decision: "There may be moreover a further fault in Wordsworth's high morality . . . which I shall characterize by the name of false or arbitrary Positiveness. There is such a thing in Morals as in all Science, as drawing your conclusion before you have properly got your premises.

It is desirable to attain a fixed point: but it is essential that the fixed point be [the] right one." [7]

Thus doubting the power of philosophical reason, unsure of how to validate what seem the claims of duty, and trusting that skepticism is not only a purer but a more likely prelude to the great revelation he desires than any affirmation, Clough clings to his doubts, using poetry as a means of exploring possible positions without committing himself to them: "Why should I say I see the things I see not,/Why be and be not?/Show love for that I love not, and fear for what I fear not?" In the poem of which these lines are the opening, Clough again states the danger of going along with the values and beliefs of those all around him. One may choose to "'keep amid the throng/. And turn as they shall turn, and bound as they are bounding," but "Alas! Alas! alas! and what if all along/The music is not sounding?" The poem then contrasts the loud but wholly illusory music with the soft inner melody which sounds only fitfully.

Finally, in one of the most impressive of the poems of *Ambarvalia*, "When Israel Came Out of Egypt," Clough uses a striking figure to carry the same burden: like those Israelites who would not wait for Moses' return, but created the Golden Calf to worship, Man in his rash impatience rushes to worship the first convenient deity rather than await the truth:

> The clouded hill attend thou still,
>   And him that went within.
> He yet shall bring some worthy thing
>   For waiting souls to see:
> Some sacred word that he hath heard
>   Their light and life shall be;
> Some lofty part, than which the heart
>   Adopt no nobler can,
> Thou shalt receive, thou shalt believe,
>   And thou shalt do, O Man!

In her "Memoir," Mrs. Clough says that "his scepticism was of no mere negative quality—not a mere rejection of tradition and denial of authority, but was the expression of a pure reverence for the inner light of the spirit, and of entire submission to its guidance." [8] This praise is not merely that of an admiring wife; it is an accurate summation of his position as developed in the early poems. Nevertheless, what Mrs. Clough does not mention is how long and weary was the watch for the inner light to shine brightly enough for Clough to make out the road he was to travel.

II *Love*

Clough's questioning in *Ambarvalia* extends not only to the nature of duty and religious truth, but also to that of true love. Clough searches for the signs, the certifying marks, as it were, of the essence of love. As in his questioning of how to recognize duty or distinguish the true attributes of the deity, it is essentially an epistemological question Clough raises. His need is not to know what the essence of love is; that would be finally as presumptuous as to ask the essence of God. What he wishes rather is a way of distinguishing the effect produced by an ideal and essential love from that produced by sheer sexual drive or romantic fancy. Perhaps to the modern temper Clough may seem to have made a radical mistake in assuming that there is indeed an isolable something which is love, but one must remember that he is speaking directly out of the Christian Platonic tradition which assumes that there exists a love ordained by God to purify man, to set his feet on the steps which lead to the vision in which the good, the true, and the beautiful blend into one.

Clough's idealism about love is seen in "With graceful seat and skilful hand," "The Silver Wedding," and to some extent in "God be with You!" (ὁ θεὸς μετὰ σοῦ). The first two especially express the ennobling and purifying powers of love and marriage. But against these more or less occasional pieces must be set three more searching poems. "Ah what is love, our love, she said," questions whether all human love and the poet's expression of idyllic love are not indeed illusions. "When panting sighs" and "*Natura Naturans*" give form to the doubts thus expressed, pursuing analysis in strange ways which must have caused readers of the time to murmur " 'Twere to consider too curiously, to consider so." The former poem asks whether what seems the delicious thrill of love is a prelude to the love of which the angels sing, or merely the "same song" the beasts know, modified only in that the "soul and spirit add/To pleasures, even base and bad,/A zest the soulless never had"—a speculation which sounds curiously like an anticipation of the ironic *fin de siècle* discussion Richard Le Gallienne later gave of decadence as adding the joys of corrupting the soul to those of corrupting the body.[9] The idealism with which Clough invests love causes him to be wary and suspicious. The question which "When panting sighs" poses is simply whether the particular complex of emotions there described measures up to the vision of ideal love. Reason is called in to speak to the question, but how can reason distinguish the "halo of the soul" from the: "Phosphoric exhalation bred/Of vapour, steaming from the bed/Of Fancy's brook or Passion's river"?

One must always bear in mind that Clough was using poetry as a means of clarifying to himself questions, problems, and possible answers; otherwise, the multitude of viewpoints suggested in the poems of *Ambarvalia* appears chaotic. In the midst of the many poems which try to separate the ideal from the impure and earthy, one of Clough's most lyrical and intensely vivid poems, "Natura Naturans," denies the premise of a radical difference between the ideal and the mundane, asserting that human love between the sexes is indeed part of a universal sexual force. The poem is startling coming from Clough's pen, for it identifies the passing pleasures of a young man and woman sitting beside each other "in casual second class" with the force operative in "Hymen's shrine" and with "The Power which e'en in stones and earths/By blind election felt, in forms/Organic breeds to myriad births." The sensations of sexual attraction are described as the flowering within each of the full force of nature:

> Flashed flickering forth fantastic flies,
>   Big bees their burly bodies swung,
> Rooks roused with civic din the elms,
>   And lark its wild reveillez rung;
> In Libyan dell the light gazelle,
>   The leopard lithe in Indian glade,
> And dolphin, brightening tropic seas,
>   In us were living, leapt and played:

Before its close, the poem has doubly accounted for the whole phenomenon: first, in terms of a guarded evolutionary theory; second, in terms of a somewhat heretical account of the "primal prime embrace" in the garden of Eden.

Of course not all the poems of *Ambarvalia* take philosophical or theological problems as their center. Such a poem as "On Latmos" (ἐπὶ Λάτμῳ), for instance, is a conventional handling of the

Endymion-Selene legend; but, while not a poem of which Clough had any reason to be ashamed, it, like most of his writing which does not bear directly on an intellectual problem, is slacker in both thought and technique than that which derives its interest from a tension between points of view. One of Clough's biographers, Lady Chorley, had indeed pronounced that " 'On Latmos' can surely be read only as a personal love poem," referring to it again as "that mysterious poem whose source and object elude conjecture." [10] As has been seen, there is some evidence for thinking that Clough may have experienced a love affair around 1846–47, but whether or no "On Latmos" was inspired by it, the poem does not, when considered by itself, convey a sense of personal passion. The same is true of "God be with you" for which the claim of a personal emotional inspiration seems even stronger. These and the few other poems in the volume which do not deal directly with intellectual conflict tend to stand out by contrast with the majority not because they express strong personal sentiments but because they seem pale and conventional.

III   *The Ongoing Debate*

Unlike Tennyson, Clough was unequal to or uninterested in taking a scene or an old legend as the subject of a poem and creating an esthetically beautiful object from it—"The Kraken," "Mariana," and "Tithonus" were outside his poetic range. Indeed, though he somewhat ambiguously vindicated the reality of poetic imagination in "Is it true, ye gods?" in another poem, "A golden key on the tongue," Clough expresses his reservations about devoting one's life to poetry. If a sense of happiness and human kindliness comes amid our "cheerless wanderings," it is not, he says, to be wasted on "the trifler, Poesy":

> Heaven grant the manlier heart, that timely, ere
> Youth fly, with life's real tempest would be coping,
>   The fruit of dreamy hoping
>   Is, waking, blank despair.

The sense of the seriousness of life which here causes him to wonder if life is not of too great import to devote much of it to poetry underlies Clough's impatience with all that is superficial, illusory, and less than of sterling goodness and truth. The same impulse

leads him in "Look you, my simple friend" to find the evil and the
crime that lead men to recognize God through his anger to be
preferable to devoting one's life to the exercise of mere wit and
cleverness.

Thus, lying beneath the variously inconsistent themes of the
poems of *Ambarvalia,* we find Clough's dedication to the serious
duties of life, to the necessity of waiting for insight and revelation,
and to the refusal to accept any emotional or intellectual coin
without subjecting it to a rigorous, if finally inconclusive, examination. But with man's duties not yet fully identified, the infallible
signs of emotional and intellectual truth not yet discovered, and
the revelation not yet come, it is hardly surprising that Clough
gave the title "Blank Misgivings of a Creature moving about in
Worlds not realized" to the sequence of ten poems which sum up
the anxieties felt during the ten years at Oxford. (All ten appear
in the 1839–42 Notebook.) The note which runs through the
whole group is repentance, but it is a repentance that does not
quite ring true because the poems are far too abstract, too speculative, to suggest that any real sin is being reflected upon:

> So in they came,
> A noisy band of revellers,—vain hopes,
> Wild fancies, fitful joys; and there they sit
> In my heart's holy place, and through the night
> Carouse. . . .
>   (31)

Such lines sound as false as similar ones of Oscar Wilde, but for
a rather different reason: one doubts Wilde's repentance, but one
doubts Clough's sins. But the tone of Clough's anxious questioning comes through convincingly enough. Through many of
these poems also runs the metaphor of debt, expressing the fear
that to enjoy life before finding and entering upon one's duties is
to incur an enormous debt, as well as to lose the hoped-for higher
insights. The tenth poem of the group, beginning "I have seen
higher holier things than these,/And therefore must to these refuse my heart" comes only to an uneasy resolution when it affirms
"Do thou, as best thou mayst, thy duty do:/Amid the things allowed thee live and love" with the promise that the Summum Pul-
chrum will yet be seen (34). The answer seems as provisional as
the others that Clough has essayed in *Ambarvalia.*

Read as completely serious statements, many of the lines in
these ten poems exaggerate the desperation of Clough's mood;
actually their seriousness is leavened with irony. The Wordsworthian echoes are at least partially lighthearted, and the source
of the title suggests that Clough was perhaps attempting to follow
Wordsworth in constructing a poem that, like the "Ode," would
work through a series of doubts and questionings to a limited
affirmation. More direct evidence that Clough did not intend by
his "Creature moving about in Worlds not realized" so desperate a
situation as that Arnold described by the similar phrase "between
two worlds" appears in a letter to Gell written in 1844. Clough
touches upon his doubts in a serious yet ironic vein which shows
him able to regard his own perplexities with objectivity:

. . . whether the Spirit of the Age, whose lacquey and flunkey I
submit to be, will prove to be this kind or that kind I can't the least
say. Sometimes I have doubts whether it won't turn out to be no Xty
at all. Also it is a more frequent question with me whether the Master
whom I work under and am content to work under is not carrying out
his operations elsewhere, while I am as it were obeying the directions
of a bungling journeyman no better than myself. As the great Goethe
published in his youth The Sorrows of the Young Werter, so may I,
you see, the great poet that am to be, publish my "Lamentations of
a Flunkey out of place." You, perhaps, will say the lamentations are
more out of place than the Flunkey. And certainly Flunkey hath no
intention of giving notice to quit just at present, nor of publishing
Lamentation at all.[11]

"Lamentations of a Flunkey out of place" could well serve as a
self-satirizing version of the title "Blank Misgivings of a Creature
moving about in Worlds not realized," and the reference to
Goethe's *The Sorrows of Werther* not only carries the implication
that Clough thinks of himself as going through a temporary stage
of thought but echoes an ironic passage from Carlyle's *Sartor* with
which Clough would have been acquainted: "Thus must he [Teu-
felsdröckh], over the whole surface of the Earth (by footprints),
write his *Sorrows of Teufelsdröckh;* even as the great Goethe, in
passionate words, had to write his *Sorrows of Werther,* before the
spirit freed herself, and he could become a man." [12] Clough's delight in literary allusion, and perhaps in finding hopeful analogues
to his own case, surely has the upper hand over despair here.

There are at least eight poems included in the Oxford edition which were written during the same years as those which appeared in *Ambarvalia* but did not find their way into that volume. Almost all of these touch on serious personal topics and echo in one way or another the themes of *Ambarvalia*; but, for the most part, they do not come up to the level of those included in that volume. Two however, deserve particular notice. "Truth is a golden thread" describes Truth, in more vivid imagery than Clough had been wont to use, as appearing only in "bright specks" though underlying all life like a vein of ore—one more attempt to explain the difficulty of discovering the Truth, this time with emphasis on the need for alertness in responding to the partial glimpses rather than waiting for a full revelation. More important is the now well-known "Epi-Strauss-ium" with its bold acceptance of the rational criticism of the Bible which has made the place of worship, "if less richly, more sincerely bright."

The reviews of *Ambarvalia,* though not entirely damning, were almost unanimous in finding Cloughs' poems too obscure and too fragmentary.[13] The expectations of the reviewers were, of course, that a poem should be a finished artifact, polished in expression, rounded in form, lucid in content, and unambiguous in point of view. We recognize today that the surface of a good poem may very well at first appear disorganized; and we can also see, looking back, that a good many Victorian poems were less unambiguous than they were thought to be. Modern readers have, moreover, been led by the whole trend of twentieth-century poetry to feel that a little obscurity is no bad thing in a poem. For these reasons, we may very well feel that Clough was simply ahead of his critics' appreciation. However, the reviewers were not speaking simply for the peculiar critical standards of their time; instead, they were championing one perennial kind of poetry over another: that which creates beauty, not that which simply attempts to express with absolute fidelity an individual response to life. It is the second goal we must value if we are to appreciate Clough, and it is only honest to admit that Clough rarely produces the first type, and almost never that highest kind of poetry which combines both.

It was perhaps his devotion to an absolute, almost philosophic, accuracy of phrasing that prevented Clough from often forging the memorable lines and phrases one recalls from other poets' works. The quotation of brief passages from Clough generally suggests a degree of prosaicness not felt when the poems from which they are taken are read complete—the delights of his poetry come not from his abilities as a phrase maker, but from his ability to convey with integrity the breadth and depth of the questions on which his intellect has been brought to bear.

At the time he was writing his poems, Clough himself was probably too much preoccupied with the process of objectifying his intellectual conflicts in poetry to worry about the world's evaluation of it; and at the time of the publication of *Ambarvalia* he was too relieved at having conclusively made his decision to leave Oxford to care much about the reviewers. The response of the world, or even of his friends, to his poetry presumably troubled him much less than his sense of loneliness in having travelled so considerable a distance from the convictions of his friends. *Sic Itur* and *Qua Cursum Ventus*—the latter one of his best-known poems (it probably records the termination of close friendship with W. G. Ward)—testify to his sense of sadness at the parting of intellectual ways and to his faith that men honestly pursuing truth may have to pursue different paths ("To veer, how vain! On, onward strain"). But the very honesty and integrity which compel them to differ may well see them through to the same goal:

> One port, methought, alike they sought,
>   One purpose hold where'er they fare,—
> O bounding breeze, O rushing seas!
>   At last, at last, unite them there!

CHAPTER 4

Amours: *An Epistolary Novel in Hexameters*

Amours de Voyage was written, at least in rough form, in the late spring and early summer of 1849 while Clough was in Italy. Like the *Bothie, Amours* tells in hexameters a story of a love affair encountered by a young man while travelling. The resemblance goes little further, for the genial good spirits of the earlier poem give way to a sharp irony, the humorously punctuated discussion about social and economic beliefs to searching introspection, and the happy outcome to a resigned acceptance of defeat.

That Clough was writing to satisfy a somewhat specialized literary palate in *Amours* is hardly a debatable proposition. The title, though more promising than that of the *Bothie,* is not especially appealing, the much-damned hexameter is again employed, the tale ends in a way which could hardly fail to annoy a great many readers, and the clumsy epistolary form is chosen as the means to get the story told. This method of narration is of course quite uneconomical since a considerable amount of material unrelated to forwarding the plot must be included if the letters are to have any degree of verisimilitude. Thus, though Clough shows considerable skill in making that which is not directly relevant to the story at least helpful in understanding Claude's character, undeniably tedious passages remain. The hexameter contributes to the sense of tediousness simply because, to the English ear, it lacks the tautness of the customary decasyllabic or shorter line. On the other hand, the hexameters of *Amours* are not so often awkward as those of the *Bothie.* The syntax is less involuted, and the annoying inversions and repetitions are avoided; most important, there are fewer lines which resist scansion and outrage one's sense of an underlying metrical pattern.

I *The Action*

A narrative poem constructed on an epistolary framework, *Amours* tells a simple story. Claude, a somewhat supercilious and oversensitive young Englishman touring on the Continent, finds himself in Rome in the company of a middle-class English family of whom he is at first scornful. Then he discovers that he may possibly be falling in love with Mary, one of the daughters. Much debate goes on in his mind as to whether he is really in love; offended by an inquiry about his intentions, he decides not to accompany the family when it leaves Rome; several days after the family's departure, he makes up his mind to follow, becoming, as he unsuccessfully tries to discover where it has gone, more and more certain that he is indeed in love with Mary; at last, forced to give up the pursuit, he begins to console himself with the thought that perhaps he had not really been in love at all.

The action of the poem, what there is of it, is clearly a fiction invented by Clough; but there is nevertheless much in the poem which suggests the autobiographical. The historical event around which the poem is built—the siege of Mazzini's Roman Republic —occurred during the time Clough actually was in Rome. Using the epistolary form in a manner reminiscent of Richardson, its English founder, Clough chronicled in detail the doubts, hesitations, and mental turmoil of the central character. The topics around which these doubts and speculations cluster, and the whole nature of the scruples and form of argument in Claude's letters look back to the poems of *Ambarvalia* and forward to *Dipsychus*.[1] Moreover, the accent of discontent which runs through the whole poem is not unlike Clough's own attitude as reflected in his letters of this time.

A year and a half had passed since his resignation of the Oriel tutorship, and the joy he had felt in escaping from the XXXIX Articles must largely have evaporated as he faced his new position in London without enthusiasm, especially since religious issues had already clouded his negotiations with the council of University Hall. He had left Oxford but found no Elspie, no work which he could fully give himself to, and no secret or clue to life in the "outer" world. (Curiously, *Amours* also anticipates the doubts and misgivings to which Clough found himself subjected during his courtship more than two years later.)

It is necessary, then, for the reader who knows something of Clough's life and other works to remember that the poet is anatomizing the mind of a man incapacitated for almost all action by the doubts and qualifications which hedge about his every thought and impulse, and that, however easy Clough found it to draw such a mind by looking into his own, it would be dangerous to take the *Amours* as a self-portrait. It is even more dangerous to take isolated phrases or lines out of their context in *Amours* and use them as examples of Clough's thought: the poem presents a series of psychological changes and reversals in the central character; that character's views are thus necessarily inconsistent. It is impossible for us to know which, if any, of Claude's statements Clough would have unqualifiedly endorsed.

On the other hand, Clough offers no corrective to Claude's intellectual dyspepsia, no vision of life implicit or explicit as a substitute (almost certainly he could not at this time have done so, but that is aside from the point here). It therefore would seem safe enough to assume that what Clough wishes the reader to see is not so much the error of Claude's intellectual stance but the ease with which the conscientious mind, especially perhaps but not exclusively as manifested in his own generation, can fall into the morass of an all-dissolving skepticism, and the manner in which the questing mind which does not find at least one firm point of belief must necessarily find all questions unresolvable. We may well read the poem, then, as Clough's investigation of a mind analogous to his own: the form of Claude's thought, its manner of treating a problem, can be assumed to be very much like Clough's, although the tentative propositions and conclusions the poem proposes do not necessarily reproduce Clough's own ponderings.

The poem opens with Claude's descriptions of his feelings about Rome. His character, as it comes through in the opening section, is thoughtful, with a kind of heatless curiosity; he is almost totally without enthusiasm. He is disappointed in Rome, and would like to understand the reasons which lie behind this reaction. While conscientiously "studying" art and monuments, he is not nearly so interested in following any question about art or history to a conclusion as in analyzing his own feelings and responses. His attitude toward the drama of the Mazzini Republic is the same: he observes all political events with an eye primarily fascinated by his own responses, making little effort to get at the facts behind charges and countercharges.

These first letters very well illustrate the difficulties of any attempt to decide when Claude can safely be taken as a spokesman for Clough. Claude's disappointment with Rome is very much like that which Clough announces in a letter to his mother soon after his arrival in Rome, even to the use of some of the same phrases and of the word "rubbishy" to sum up Rome's general effect. Various other letters express an indecision about whether to remain in Rome that is also quite like Claude's.[2] On the other hand, the whole tone is exaggerated in Claude's letters, seemingly as a means of emphasizing his mental malaise. And then there is the passionate attack on the Jesuits and the influence of Spanish Catholicism:

> Luther was foolish,—but, O great God! what call you Igna-
> tius?
> O my tolerant soul, be still! but you talk of barbarians,
> Alaric, Attila, Genseric;—why, they came, they killed, they
> Ravaged, and went on their way; but these vile, tyrannous
> Spaniards,
> These are here still,—how long, O ye heavens, in the country
> of Dante?
> . . . .
> Here with emasculate pupils and gimcrack churches of Gesu,
> Pseudo-learning and lies, confessional boxes and postures,—
> (180)

Clough's own feelings are not unlikely to have been similar—after all, one who found endorsement of the XXXIX Articles prejudicial to true religious revelation was unlikely to see value in the more rigorous dogma of Catholicism or in its elaborate external expression. However, nothing in Clough's other writing gives warrant for attributing to him a view of such violence and intolerance; and, moreover, the passage has a thematic function in showing the combination of strength and impotence in Claude's religious sentiments. That which offends him by expressing itself in terms which seem to deviate too extremely from true religious feeling receives all his scorn; but he has no doctrine, faith, or ceremony to which he can give his own assent.

Something of Claude's cultural snobbishness is also to be found
in Clough's letters, a dislike for, or at least suspicion of, the man-
ners of the shopkeeping middle class. But again the attitude given
Claude is a substantial exaggeration of Clough's own feelings. The
situation at the beginning of *Amours* is not unlike that in *Pride
and Prejudice:* like D'Arcy, Claude is to find that his pride can
stoop to love a girl from the middle class; and, like Elizabeth Ben-
ton, Mary is to find that Claude is not so selfish, cold, and proud
as she had once thought. Beneath the pride and prejudice on the
part of both Miss Austen's characters there are resolution and
common sense, but Claude lacks the quality of resolute decisive-
ness. In addition to presenting Claude in a position from which he
must retreat, Claude's comments on the Trevellyn family serve to
show the fastidiousness which is one of the roots of his irresolution. Thus the rather unattractive personality revealed as Claude
makes scornful fun of these friends and acquaintances, who are
very convenient for him at this point, serves several purposes:

> Not that I like them much or care a *bajocco* for Vernon,
> But I am slow at Italian, have not many English acquaint-
>   ance,
> And I am asked, in short, and am not good at excuses.
> Middle-class people these, bankers very likely, not wholly
> Pure of the taint of the shop; will at table d'hôte and res-
>   taurant
> Have their shilling's worth, their penny's pennyworth even:
> Neither man's aristocracy this, nor God's, God knoweth!
>   (181)

On the other hand, in the next scene Claude is shown in a much
more sympathetic light as he turns his critical analysis ironically
on himself:

> Dear, dear, what do I say? But, alas, just now, like Iago,
> I can be nothing at all, if it is not critical wholly;
> So in fantastic height, in coxcomb exaltation,
> Here in the Garden I walk, can freely concede to the Maker
> That the works of his hand are all very good: his creatures,
> Beast of the field and fowl, he brings them before me; I
>   name them;
> That which I name them, they are,—the bird, the beast, and
>   the cattle.

> But for Adam,—alas, poor critical coxcomb Adam!
> But for Adam there is not found an help-meet for him.
>
> (181)

But these prejudices, opinions, and general speculations are not
of central interest and importance in the poem. The endless circle
of doubts, questioning, and swampy speculation in such a mind as
Claude's truly begins only when it is confronted by a practical
decision. Claude's tentative recognition that he is beginning to
think of Mary as a possible wife stirs and muddies the mental
waters. Having already experienced the agonies of trying to find
solid ground for making decisions, Claude can anticipate the outcome of his entering into closer relationships with the Trevellyns.
In letter twelve of Canto I, he writes to Eustace:

> Yes, I am going,—I feel and cannot recall it,—
> Fusing with this thing and that, entering into all sorts of
> relations,
> Tying I know not what ties which, whatever they are, I
> know one thing,
> Will, and must, woe is me, be one day painfully broken.
>
> (184)

Using the imagery of a dive into the ocean to suggest the plunge
into a fuller participation in life, Claude foresees in the latter lines
of the letter that he will be borne back up out of the sea as by a
rope and "Look yet abroad from the height o'er the sea whose salt
I have tasted." One ironical phrase in this letter clearly foretells
the outcome of the poem which Emerson, among others, so dep-
recated: even in the midst of his romantic feelings, Claude expresses his preference for "the great massy strengths of abstraction" which are for him firmer than the sea of experience or the
pressure of the emotions.

The complexity and emotional disturbance of Claude's debates
with himself vary, naturally enough, with the strength of the impulse toward, or the necessity of, making a decision. The cool
irony of the often-quoted passage in which Claude discusses dying for a cause is possible precisely because such a course of
action is not seriously suggesting itself to him:

> *DULCE* it is, and *decorum*, no doubt, for the country to
> fall,—to

Offer one's blood an oblation to Freedom, and die for the
    Cause; yet
Still, individual culture is also something, and no man
Finds quite distinct the assurance that he of all others is
    called on,
Or would be justified, even, in taking away from the world
    that
Precious creature, himself. Nature sent him here to abide
    here,
Else why sent him at all? Nature wants him still, it is likely.

. . . .

Sweet it may be and decorous, perhaps, for the country to
    die; but,
On the whole, we conclude the Romans won't do it, and I
    shan't.

(188)

Again Claude's ironical question of whether he is prepared to be a
martyr "for the British female," a question not generated by a
strong sense of the likelihood of the need, is conducted with more
wit than seriousness, though the raising of a corollary question as
to whether a man can presume beforehand that he will be ready
when the time comes is an indication of a greater uneasiness than
in the former instance.

But, having accepted the possiblity of falling fully in love with
Mary, and having therefore to take decisive action, Claude finds
the sluice gates of extensive and curious speculation open. Is his
feeling produced by mere juxtaposition, and is Mary to be taken
to wife for the same reason one talks "with the girl that is next
one"—to lighten the tedium? (The difference between this coldly
rational questioning and the Romantic idealism underlying the
use of a similar scene in "*Natura Naturans*" is, whether intentional
or not, striking.) Is marriage "pours passer le temps" in this life:

But for his funeral train which the bridegroom sees in the
    distance,
Would he joyfully, think you, fall in with the marriage-
    procession?
But for that final discharge, would he dare to enlist in that
    service?

(202–03)

Is there ever a true affinity between lovers or only juxtaposition and "the law of the land and the ruinous force of the will"? Is the care with which Mary has avoided giving him the feeling that he has any obligation to her proof of her innocence or of her cunning?

Such questions, not likely to draw to an end of themselves, are made irrelevant when the choice is no longer possible. When Mary and her family leave Rome without Claude, a sense of boredom and emptiness forces him to pursue her. "*ACTION will furnish belief,*" writes Claude to Eustace in the midst of his search for the Trevellyns; and, though he immediately adds "but will that belief be the true one?", he is, for the moment, committed. But, once the immediate action has proved fruitless and additional action must be taken, doubts are again possible. In the midst of regret and hopes that he will still encounter her, a part of his mind begins to ask if resignation to circumstance is not the wisest course; and the word "factitious" begins to appear amidst Claude's musings as he increasingly fears that any affirmation he might make must be less than honest. Then, in the fifth letter of the last canto, a significant identification emerges as Claude for a moment thinks of Mary almost as an unobtainable Beatrice who is summoning him toward faith, "religious assurance," and "the Absolute": "Yet if I do but aspire evermore to the Absolute only,/I shall be doing, I think, somehow, what she will be doing;—" (215).

But this mood also passes; in the fragments which make up the fifth letter, Claude rejects as "factitious" the momentary insight, and records in more emotionally charged language than appears anywhere else in the poem the crisis in which he does finally make a decisive commitment—not to commit himself to any sort of faith:

> What with trusting myself and seeking support from within
> me,
> Almost I could believe I had gained a religious assurance,
> Found in my own poor soul a great moral basis to rest on.
> Ah! but indeed I see, I feel it factitious entirely:
> I refuse, reject, and put it utterly from me;
> I will look straight out, see things, not try to evade them;
> Fact shall be fact for me, and the Truth the Truth as ever,

Flexible, changeable, vague, and multiform, and doubtful.—
Off, and depart to the void, thou subtle, fanatical tempter!

I shall behold thee again (is it so?) at a new visitation,
O ill genius thou! I shall, at my life's dissolution,
(When the pulses are weak, and the feeble light of the
    reason
Flickers, an unfed flame retiring slow from the socket),
Low on a sick-bed laid, hear one, as it were, at the doorway,
And looking up see thee, standing by, looking emptily at me;
I shall entreat thee then, though now I dare to refuse thee,—
Pale and pitiful now, but terrible then to the dying.—
Well, I will see thee again: and while I can, will repel thee.

Claude's psychic bankruptcy is now complete—any urge to
commit himself, emotionally or intellectually, to any faith, ideal,
or person, even to a wife, he regards as a tempter to be resisted
with all his strength. Thus, when the long hoped-for letter arrives
giving the names of the friends of the Trevellyn family who may
know its whereabouts, Claude has passed the point of taking action. His earlier ironical self, holding above all involvement, has
already begun to return. In the sixth letter, consciously realizing
the ludicrous contrast between his own egoistic struggles and
those of the now-fallen Roman republic, he plays with the question of whether "the souls of the brave that die in the battle" perish with their cause, are borne up "on the slumberous pinions of
angels," or remain "haunting the grave of their by-gone hope and
endeavour." He can answer only "Whither depart the brave?—
God knows; I certainly do not."

Claude can now doubt all his earlier feelings—"After all perhaps there was something factitious about it"—and return to a
kind of drifting life, taking action only as circumstance absolutely
requires: "Ah, the key of our life, that passes all wards, opens all
locks,/Is not *I will*, but *I must*" (218). There follows a passage
some twenty lines later which, though it states the same acquiescence in Providence as Philip's in the final section of the *Bothie,*
contrasts markedly in its pessimism with the tone of the earlier
passage: "What is ordained is right, and all that happens is or-
dered./Ah, no, that isn't it. But yet I retain my conclusion./I will
go where I am led, and will not dictate to chances."

The last letter announces Claude's return to his quest for

knowledge, vain and sterile as that has proved for him in the past. His earlier description of Knowledge as a "needless, unfruitful blossom" set in the top of the Tree of Life, where it decays even as it flowers, denied the possibilities of rational thought too strongly; the position to which he has now come errs in the other direction: "Not as the Scripture says, is, I think, the fact. Ere our death-day,/Faith, I think, does pass, and Love; but Knowledge abideth." That resolution, combined with Claude's inability to rest in any resolution, casts a shadow of discontent over Claude's future; one's final impression includes little sense of the new strength in Claude which Clough, on the evidence of at least one letter, seemingly wished to represent.[3]

II *Claude's Problem*

In *Amours,* as elsewhere, Clough vividly portrays a mind recoiling from action because of fear of error. The action decided upon may prove to be mistaken. However, as Henry Sidgwick pointed out in a letter to Mrs. Clough, Claude's inaction is partially the result of his idealism or "philosophic" devotion to knowledge. Sidgwick distinguishes between Claude's distaste for "the mode of selection" and "the fact of selection."[4] Claude questions the mode in which he is selecting Mary—are his feelings for her the result merely of juxtaposition? But he is equally troubled by the fact— the necessity—of selection, for it commits one to leaving the realm of sympathetic contemplation of all that is attractive in the world and descending to selfish interests and "petty particular doings."

In the first instance, Claude is held back by a timidity in regard to action which results from the uncertainty about himself engendered by his skeptical speculations. In the second, the same reluctance to abandon the purity of uncalculating contemplation implied in the poems of *Ambarvalia* operates. In the sixth letter of Canto III, in the midst of lamenting that a woman demands to be loved to the exclusion of a man's dedication to highest ideals, Claude laments that she cannot be told "That in the end she shall yield to a perfect and absolute something,/Which I then for myself shall behold, and not another." The point is reinforced by the half-ironic but also half-serious allusion to Job XIX: 27 in the second line: the "fact of selection" is inimicable to the ideal vision. A key letter is the eighth of Canto III. Rising above his ironic comment on those he sees "consorting and coupling," Claude finds life

momentarily beautiful; and so it would continue "could we elimi-
nate only/This vile hungering impulse, this demon within us of
craving." The desires which draw one into participation in life,
however one tries to purify them, destroy the contemplative
vision.

If Sidgwick's observations have perhaps here been developed beyond his intentions, evidence for this interpretation may be found
in two lines, not included in the standard text, the importance of
which has been pointed out by Richard Gollin: "It is the virtue of
man to know and love the ideal./It is the wisdom of man to
accept and love the real." [5]

III   *The Prologues and Epilogues*

Despite Claude's constant mental revaluation and the intense
emotional reaction which breaks through in the fifth letter of
Canto V, the letters which make up the body of the poem are
generally straightforward enough, and the story emerges from
them with perfect clarity. But there is one puzzling portion of the
poem which has nowhere received comment: the lyrical prefaces
and epilogues to each canto. The relationship of a number of
these to the tale proper is not at all clear, principally because they
are not consistently spoken by the same voice. Of the ten passages, all the epilogues and three of the prologues can without
difficulty be attributed to the narrator, but the whole of one prologue and at least a portion of another would seem rather the
direct comments of Claude.

The prologue to Canto I is an invitation:

> Over the great windy waters, and over the clear-crested sum-
> mits,
>   Unto the sun and the sky, and unto the perfecter earth,
> Come, let us go,—to a land wherein gods of the old time
> wandered,
>   Where every breath even now changes to ether divine.
>   (177)

The "we" in such invitational openings conventionally refers to
narrator and reader, and so it seems here. Incidentally, the narrator, by the fifth line, has already qualified his invitation with the
skeptical reflection that changing the surrounding scene does not
change the individual. The reader is thus warned at the outset

that Claude will remain Claude and that, whenever the poem drifts toward romanticism, it will be jerked back by a skeptical realism.

The "I" of the epilogue of Canto I seems also to be the narrator despite the shift from first-person plural to singular. One is very much tempted to take these lines as Clough's disillusioned comments on his own trip. The speaker finds himself haunted by "Alba," which seem to be the Alban hills and their mythic associations, but he cannot decide whether the feeling they engender is an imperfect vision of truth, a religious reverence, or an illusion: "So through the city I wander and question, unsatisfied ever,/Reverent so I accept, doubtful because I revere" (186). The doubt could be either Claude's or the narrator's, but it seems so little linked with the contents of Claude's letters that one is inclined to take it as that of the narrator—of Clough or a *persona* very little distanced.

Both the preface and epilogue to Canto II are also perhaps best taken as the voice of the narrator: the preface again asks whether the "spirit from perfecter ages," which seems to abide in Rome, is an illusion. The epilogue, commenting on the action, forecasts that Claude will remain in Rome seeking solace "in the Past and the Arts" but will be forced finally to follow Mary. Also easily read as the narrator's commentary are the epilogues to Cantos III and IV and the prologue to Canto V. The epilogue to Canto V, which closes the poem, also belongs to this group: it is unambiguously cast in the conventional form of the author's farewell to his work.

> So go forth to the world, to the good report and the evil!
>   Go, little book! thy tale, is it not evil and good?
> Go, and if strangers revile, pass quietly by without answer.
>   Go, and if curious friends ask of thy rearing and age,
> Say, "I am flitting about many years from brain unto brain
>   of
> Feeble and restless youths born to inglorious days:
> But," so finish the word, "I was writ in a Roman chamber,
>   When from Janiculan heights thundered the cannon of
>   France."
>
>   (220)

The prologues to Cantos III and IV do not fit the same pattern. The prologue to Canto III, beginning in the first person plural,

appears at first to be the narrator's comment on the action of that
canto: "Yet to the wondrous St. Peter's, and yet to the solemn
Rotunda,/. . . . Yet may we think, and forget, and possess our
souls in resistance." But it then breaks into a long passage evoking
the beauty of rural Italy and concludes, curiously, in the first
person singular:

> Ah, but away from the stir, shouting, and gossip of war,
> Where, upon Apennine slope, with the chestnut the oak-
>   trees immingle,
> Where amid odorous copse bridle-paths wander and wind,
> Where under mulberry-branches the diligent rivulet sparkles,
>   Or amid cotton and maize peasants their water-works ply,
> Where, over fig-tree and orange in tier upon tier still re-
>   peated,
> Garden on garden upreared, balconies step to the sky,—
> Ah, that I were, far away from the crowd and the streets of
>   the city,
> Under the vine-trellis laid, O my beloved, with thee!
>   (199)

Who is the "I"? It may be Claude; but, if so, who is speaking in
the opening half of the preface, and why the shift from "we" to
"I"? It may be the narrator; but, if so, who is the "beloved"? Finally, the prologue to Canto IV seems to speak directly for
Claude: "Eastward, or Northward, or West? I wonder and ask as
I wonder/Weary, yet eager and sure, where shall I come to my
love?" That it should seem so is puzzling since the lyrical tone of
the passage is quite different from Claude's epistolary style, and
thus it may be read as presenting the ideal or romantic ferment
which Claude consciously suppresses in his own mind. But it can
hardly be read as the narrator's voice unless one wishes to assume
not only that Clough had a romance in Italy, but that the story in
Amours is modeled *directly* on it.

Was Clough alluding to some personal experience? All accounts
point to Clough's having met Blanche in the summer of 1851, two
years after the trip to Rome. Besides the subject matter of
Amours, the only extant information that might support the assumption that Clough had a romance in Italy is Tom Arnold's
belief that Clough had undergone at that time some kind of emotional crisis.[6] One can justify no more than the barest statement of

the possibility of a romantic involvement in Italy, and the matter remains as conjectural as the possible Highland romance.

Despite the demands which the hexameter form makes on the reader, a number of recent writers have found *Amours* deserving of strong praise.[7] The poem has suffered considerably, however, from those who have regarded it primarily as a quarry from which to mine biographical clues. When it is read as the psychological study of the vicissitudes of a certain kind of mind, as Clough intended, its merits are seen to be considerable—perhaps considerable enough to merit J. D. Jump's comment that it is "one of the finest and most readable longer poems of the Victorian age."

CHAPTER 5

Inner Tension as Dialogue: Dipsychus

SET in Venice, the thirteen scenes of *Dipsychus* present the conflict between a painfully conscientious idealist—whose doubts about religious truth, the meaning of love, and his own motives make it almost impossible for him to pursue any line of action—and a mocking Spirit urging compromise, action, and the claims of pleasure. At least until the end of the nineteenth century, this work, the best-known and most congenial of Clough's longer poems to the modern reader, was passed over as an interesting but not altogether successful experiment—or, more damningly, as a very inferior imitation of Goethe's *Faust*.[1] The *Bothie*, on the other hand, was regarded as the height of his achievement. Among the reasons *Dipsychus* was so long ignored is the fact that it remained unpublished during Clough's lifetime and was also excluded from the collected edition of 1862. When it first appeared in 1865 in the privately printed *Letters and Remains of Arthur Hugh Clough,* Mrs. Clough was careful to point out its unfinished state, she having contributed to its incompleteness by excluding a number of lines.

Nevertheless, interest in Clough was strong enough for the 1869 *Poems and Prose Remains,* which reprinted *Dipsychus,* to receive a number of reviews and to attain some fourteen printings. One suspects, therefore, that perhaps the primary reason *Dipsychus* continued, with few exceptions, to be ranked below the *Bothie* was simply that the Romantic and largely lighthearted earlier poem was much more to the taste of most Victorian critics. The very astringency of tone and inconclusiveness of judgment which appeal to the mid-twentieth-century reader were found disturbing and distasteful, especially to those who knew and admired Clough and wished to minimize his reputation as a "poet of doubt."

The twentieth century has recognized in *Dipsychus* a powerful presentation of the doubt, divided allegiance, and despair which make up so large a part of its cultural atmosphere. And, in an age which appears to value irony above almost any other literary quality, Clough's ability to satirize painful intellectual struggles and to give to the mocking spirit such a witty command of language and thought that agonized conscientiousness generally comes off second best satisfies both contemporary taste and the contemporary critical dictum that irony is a guarantor of intellectual depth.

I   *The Structure*

Nevertheless, even twentieth-century commentators have missed seeing precisely where the novelty and strength of *Dipsychus* lies, as well as where the weakness and imperfections are found. In the first seven scenes, constituting more than half the poem, the conflict is much more complex than that between idealistic and corrupt sides of man's nature. Dipsychus is "two-sided" in that the moral idealist and the intellectual realist in him are constantly at odds; the Spirit, although clearly also speaking from a habitation within Dipsychus's mind, is a third voice representing worldly compromise. He is indeed a tempter, tempting Dipsychus to abandon his seemingly fruitless internal debate and live as others; but, in the first half of the poem, the position he represents could no more surely be labeled "evil" or "inspired by the devil" than could the idealistic and realistic poles within Dipsychus's mind. There is always the possibility that worldly wisdom may be correct, a possibility which is meant to haunt the reader just as it does Dipsychus. If neither of the poles of Dipsychus's intellect, an honestly skeptical realism and a fierce idealism, can prove its truth by a decisive victory over the other, one cannot wholly banish the reluctant suspicion that the compromising spirit may after all be right.

In Scene VIII, however, the underlying structure of the poem suddenly changes. The voice of Dipsychus, which has hitherto almost totally limited itself to speaking in opposition to the Spirit, now begins to speculate about and to speak directly to the Spirit, addressing him as Mephistopheles. From this point on, the tension which had existed between the two poles of Dipsychus's mind largely disappears, leaving only the conflict of a diminutive Faust with a conventional devil. Dipsychus's perplexity is reduced from the attempt to discover which is the true view of life to debating

whether or not to yield to a temptation that he is sure is evil; and
the reader suddenly has provided for him a clear antithesis between evil and good.

In Scene XIII, the Spirit acknowledges the names Cosmarchon
and Cosmocrator, to which Dipsychus replies by quoting from the
Greek Testament the passage translated in the King James version
as "the rulers of the darkness of this world" (Ephesians, VI:12).
In the prose epilogue, the poet, whether Clough or a *persona*, says
of the spirit: " 'perhaps he wasn't a devil after all. That's the beauty
of the poem; nobody can say. You see, dear sir, the thing which it
is attempted to represent is the conflict between the tender conscience and the world. Now, the over-tender conscience will, of
course, exaggerate the wickedness of the world; and the Spirit in
my poem may be merely the hypothesis or subjective imagination,
formed—' "

At this point the poet's uncle breaks in, " 'Oh, for goodness'
sake, my dear boy . . . don't go into the theory of it. If you're
wrong in it, it makes bad worse; if you're right, you may be a
critic, but you can't be a poet.' " Now the epilogue—which, according to the editors of the Oxford edition, appears at the end of the
First Revision, the revision devoted to the second half of the poem
—is clearly Clough's explanation of what he thinks he has done.[2]
According to the epilogue, the change in the role of the Spirit is
entirely a subjective phenomenon within Dipsychus's mind, and
the real nature of the Spirit is still to be regarded as ambiguous.
But the explanation does not correspond with the effect produced
in the reader, and the fact that Clough provides the uncle with
apt comment on the error of such explanation is evidence that he
was aware something was going wrong.

To be convinced that something went grievously awry in the
handling of the latter half of the poem, one need only look at the
fragment "Dipsychus Continued." Though probably not written
as a direct continuation, it is in some sense a sequel to *Dipsychus,*
though very much inferior to it. The tone has become melodramatic, the elevation of Dipsychus to Lord Chief Justice is improb-
able, and the link between the woman who returns to remind him
of his earlier sin and his later success is a tritely Faustian bargain.
Yet "Dipsychus Continued" is simply a further development of the
tendency to reduce the poem to a simplified conflict with the
Mephistopheles of the Faust legend.

Clough was never able to give coherence to the total poem. In the first draft, written in Venice in 1850, the speakers are given forms of the names "Faustulus" and "Mephistopheles." Part way through what seems the first revision, the "M." and "F." used to distinguish the speakers become "D." and "S." Since Clough is already referring to the poem as "Dipsychus" in his correspondence by December, 1852 (as the Oxford editors point out), the revision was almost certainly begun before this date.

Clough does not seem to have realized the full implications of the differences between the two sets of names. Even in the first draft "Dipsychus" and the "Spirit" are much more appropriate names for the characters who speak in the scenes which make up the first portion, and "Faustulus" and "Mephistopheles" the appropriate names in the later scenes. There is no indication in any of the revisions that Clough saw the difficulty clearly enough to begin to resolve it, and the imperfect state in which the poem was left argues his continued dissatisfaction with it. "Dipsychus Continued" was once thought to have been written long after *Dipsychus* had been put aside, and its melodramatic and conventional morality were attributed to Blanche's influence. However, Lady Chorley discovered strong evidence that the continuation was written in America and thus must be dated between November, 1852, and June, 1853;[3] the fragmentary continuation becomes, therefore, evidence that Clough was still on the wrong track as he tinkered with the poem during the months just previous to his return from America and his virtual abandonment of poetry.

Despite Clough's unhappiness at University Hall and the agonizing difficulties of finding some way of earning enough to marry Blanche, one cannot regard *Dipsychus* as having been begun in a time of unrelieved and despairing battle against the corrupt and compromising beliefs of the great world. In June, 1850, Clough had written to J. C. Shairp:

It continues to strike me how ignorant you and I and other young men of our set are. Actual life is unknown to an Oxford student, even though he is not a mere Puseyite and goes on jolly reading parties— Enter the arena of your brethren and go not to your grave without knowing what common merchants and sollicitors, much more sailors and coalheavers, are well acquainted with. Ignorance is a poor kind of innocence. The World is wiser than the wise and as innocent as the innocent: 'The Earth,' said the great traveller, 'is much the same wherever we go': and the changes of position which women and students tremble and shilly shally before, leave things much as they found them.[4]

Clough's review of F. W. Newman's *The Soul*, almost certainly written about the same time, sets forth the same doctrine:

Few persons perhaps pass the age of 30, very few males reach it, without having some how or other, by Atonement or Assurance doctrines, by confessions or sacraments, by religious hypothesis or plain common sense and carelessness, quieted their conscience, and brought their minds to the comfortable conclusion that they must get on as best they may. If they have taken any decisive step, made any irremediable religious decision, entered the pulpit, or joined some sect, in their early too-poetical rashness, it is awkward, but somehow it is managed. As the great Traveller said, the World is much the same everywhere.—Common sense permeates even into the prayer-meeting; —is even there found indispensable.[5]

There is considerable irony here—the "comfortable conclusion" deserves cautious scrutiny, and, after all, the "great Traveller" is Satan, but Clough is nevertheless serious. It almost seems that Clough had begun *Dipsychus* with the intention of approving the Spirit's counsel of submission, or that he was trying to treat a position that he had already passed through and had been driven to fall back on the conventional when he was not directly representing his own immediate strife. In any case, it is not surprising that the later portions of *Dipsychus* are inconsistent both with the opening and with the final resolution toward which his scrupulous skepticism had been slowly moving since 1850. Clough must still have been inclined now to take one view, now to take another, as suggested perhaps by events in his personal life, trying them out poetically.

II   *The Debate*

In the greater portion of *Dipsychus*, one feels, Clough is treating his intellectual conflicts more directly than in either the *Bothie* or *Amours*. There is in *Dipsychus* no fictional framework at all, but there are direct transcriptions of mental debates touched off by scenes or incidents sketched very lightly or merely hinted at. Clough could hardly have found a method of construction better

suited to his talents. Weak in the designing of plots and in deline-
ating the psychology of characters with other than Dipsychean
personalities, Clough was able to side-step these limitations and
to concentrate on what he could do best: the presentation of the
sensitive, perceptive, but unresolved mind. The opening lines, in
which Dipsychus finds himself reminded of "those old verses
. . . I made last year at Naples," tie *Dipsychus* to the poet responsible for "Easter Day." (On page 44 of the 1850 Venice notebook, in the midst of passages from *Dipsychus* appear the words
"Matthew and Mark and Luke" which begin "Epi-Strauss-ium,"
suggesting that Clough intended at one time to have Dipsychus
quote that poem also.)

What one finds, then, is Clough taking a poem he has just written as a point of departure for a renewal of the full-scale internal
debate which lay behind *Ambarvalia* and *Amours* and to some
extent the *Bothie.* There are also direct references to Clough's
own habits and experience. In Scene V the Spirit makes fun of
Dipsychus's delight in swimming:

> But you—with this one bathe, no doubt,
> Have solved all questions out and out.
> 'Tis Easter Day, and on the Lido
> Lo, Christ the Lord is risen indeed, O!
>   (255)

The dialogue in Scene VIII seems directly to reflect Clough's
strong antipathy to taking Holy Orders, and his difficulties in pursuing teaching (his lack of industry in building up University
Hall as well as his religious scruples at Oxford) lie behind the
Spirit's mocking evaluation of Dipsychus's prospects as a teacher
in Scene XI:

> Teach youth—in a small way; that is, always
> So as to have much time left for yourself;
> This you can't sacrifice, your leisure's precious.
> Heartily you will not take to anything;
> Will parents like that, think you? 'He writes poems
> He's odd opinions—hm!—and's not in Orders'—
> For that you won't be.
>   (286)

Dipsychus is indeed a *persona,* but a much more transparent one
than Philip or Claude (and indeed, the tentative intellectual positions represented in the various poems of *Ambarvalia* could well
be described as the products of Clough's adoption of a succession
of *personae*).

The use of "Easter Day" in the opening of the poem presents
one pole of Dipsychus's internal conflict: his skeptical, empirical
bent of mind assures him that Christ has not risen. The Scriptures
are not sufficient as evidence, and the sinfulness of the world assures him that it was unchanged by Christ's life or death. On the
other hand, the idealism into which his speeches again and again
break refuses to accept the skeptical conclusion. The Spirit represents the attitude behind the life led by all who simply take the
world as it is, and his mocking tone expresses not what is actually
said by the *homme moyen sensual,* but the attitude lying behind
his life—and the scorn with which Dipsychus feels the average
man would regard his own painful conscientiousness. The Spirit
speaks for the crowd as Dipsychus understands it. Thus he agrees
with Dipsychus that "at Venice/Christ is not risen either."

> Nay—
> T'was well enough once in a way;
> Such things don't fall out every day.
> Having once happened, as we know,
> In Palestine so long ago,
> How should it now at Venice here?
> Where people, true enough, appear
> To appreciate more and understand
> Their ices, and their Austrian band,
> And dark-eyed girls—
>
> (224)

In answer to Dipsychus's question about what the people of
Venice do, the Spirit replies in one of the most effective passages
given him; wit, irony, and melody combine to produce mordant
commentary:

> Enjoy the minute,
> And the substantial blessings in it;
> Ices, *par exemple;* evening air;

> Company, and this handsome square;
> Some pretty faces here and there;
>
> . . . .
>
> Singing, ye gods, and dancing too—
> Tooraloo, tooraloo, tooraloo, loo;
> Fiddle di, diddle di, diddle di da
> *Figaru sù, Figaro giù*
> *Figaro quà, Figaro là!*
> How he likes doing it! Ah ha ha!
>
> (225)

The moral and spiritual idealism of Dipsychus which he feels so
strongly, but for which there is no sure base if indeed "Christ is
not risen," is given expression in the second scene, set in the Public Garden. The Spirit, speaking for that normal degree of sensual-
ity which Dipsychus deplores in himself but cannot exorcise so
long as he is unable to resolve the two poles of his speculation,
urges attention to the charms of the pretty girls, to which Dipsychus's indignant moral idealism replies:

> Off, off! Oh heaven, depart, depart, depart!
> Oh me! the toad sly-sitting at Eve's ear
> Whispered no dream more poisonous than this!
>
> (227)

The same strongly idealistic note runs through Dipsychus's speech
in Scene IIA in which the Spirit, advancing a variety of arguments, pursues his invitation to sexual experience. The most significant of the Spirit's attacks is the charge that Dipsychus expects
from sexual experience "a revelation, a mystic mouthful that will
give/Knowledge and death—none know and live!" Moral values
aside, Clough is asking whether such a being as Dipsychus—as
himself—does not expect from all action and choice a revelation,
either of truth or of his own damnation. Clearly one who sees the
stakes so high will be hesitant in all things. The lines are also
typical of Clough's very delicate use of allusion—here, of course,
the fatal apple in the garden of Eden lies beneath the Spirit's
phrasing.

Fear of irretrievable action and of compromise is the natural
result of Dipsychus's deep uncertainty about the meaning of reli-

gion, the nature of love, the grounds of duty, and, in short, about
the nature of all experience. The problem is that which underlies
the poems of *Ambarvalia,* and Dipsychus's solution is the same
suggested by the sum of those poems: to keep all alternatives
open, to maintain a kind of absolute purity by refusing to make
any decisions. There are, however, three very important differences between the debates and speculations in *Dipsychus* and
those in *Ambarvalia.* First, there seems no longer any expectation
that the long refusal to act or make decisions will be rewarded by
a vision of the true or the good. Second, as a kind of corollary,
where poems in *Ambarvalia* reveal a series of attempts to come to
terms with doubt and questioning, the speeches of *Dipsychus*
concern themselves more and more with the problem of taking
action, all hope of finding answers seemingly having been given
up. But, third, *all* courses of action are now seen as inseparable
from worldly compromise and corruption. Dipsychus discusses society as if its whole fabric were based on complaisance, deceit,
and disingenuousness, especially in Scene III and in the closing
section, and he regards all professions as corrupt and dishonest, as
sent by the Spirit of worldliness, or, as he has become by the last
section, Mephistopheles. Even to propose marriage would require
the Spirit's aid.

Moreover, a well-known passage in Scene V suggests Dipsychus's realization that, even if he were to accept the conclusion to
which his "Christ is not risen" leads, life would be not merely
without meaning but a cheat and a fraud in which no course of
action would find sanction: "If work's a cheat, so's pleasure
too;/And nothing's new and nothing's true." The Spirit later comments that there is a "strong Strauss-smell" about "Easter Day,"
but Dipsychus is unable to rise to Strauss's new religion.

Dipsychus's speech in Scene IX—in which he sums up his despair of finding direction or consolation in religion, his doubts of
the possibility of finding true love, and his fear of either action or
inaction—is the turning point, to the extent there is one, in the
poem. (It is interesting to note that in the midst of this speech,
Dipsychus seems to blame the modern age for his inability to act
since he refers to the modern Hotspur who "consults columns in a
railway guide," but this complaint soon dissolves into a general
arraignment of the condition of the individual life which is time-

less in its burdens.) From this point on, though Dipsychus vacil-
lates, his submission to the spirit is assured.

That submission, however, appears very curious when one begins to question what it is to which Dipsychus is to submit. The
Spirit is never very explicit about his demands, but they appear to
be no more than the relinquishment of speculation and the adoption of some line of action. Though, as remarked above, Dipsychus has throughout the poem equated action with worldly compromise, and now, in the latter portion with the devil's designs,
this conclusion is surely a strange one. Dipsychus's earlier scruples
are now endorsed completely, for surely the argument in Scene
XII in which Dipsychus rationalizes his decision is meant to appear utterly specious to the reader:

> If I submit, it is but to gain time
> And arms and stature: 'tis but to lie safe
> Until the hour strike to arise and slay.
>   (289)

Walter Bagehot, who knew Clough, has reported Clough's distrust for the abstract: "Reconcile what you have to say with green
peas, for green peas are certain; such was Mr. Clough's idea." [6]
Clough's presentation of Dipsychus's mind as dwelling too much in
the ideal and abstract can, then, be read as an implicit criticism of
Dipsychus's whole position—and self-criticism of his own intellectual habits. Scene IV, which finds Dipsychus and the Spirit in a
gondola, weaves Dipsychus's romantic revery, inspired by the
light, soft movement of the gondola, with the passages of the Spirit's cynical wit and of his own misgivings when the real intrudes.
Only in the latter part of the poem does the contrast break down
—perhaps intentionally, in accordance with the view of the poem
stated in the epilogue—but to the detriment of the "edge" and
tension felt to this point.

III   *Poetic Mastery*

However one may regret that Dipsychus arrives at no more
satisfactory conclusion, the poem must be granted its place as the
apex of Clough's technical achievement. The colloquial tone
which he has sought in much of his poetry, especially in the

Bothie (where the effect is of a roughness perversely beyond the colloquial), is successfully captured; the speeches of Dipsychus and the Spirit are perfectly differentiated. Beyond the mechanical opposition of the Spirit's crisp couplets against the blank verse and occasional hexameters of Dipsychus, there is also the opposition between Dipsychus's constant tendency to move toward abstract generalities and trite phrases and the Spirit's grasp of the palpable world. One may compare Dipsychus's

> O welcome then, the sweet domestic bonds,
> The matrimonial sanctities; the hopes
> And cares of wedded life; parental thoughts,
> The prattle of young children, the good word
> Of fellow men. . . .
>
> (232)

with the Spirit's

> These juicy meats, this flashing wine,
>   May be an unreal mere appearance;
> Only—for my inside, in fine
>   They have a singular coherence.
>   (241)

Despite the seriousness of the poem's theme, Clough seems to be enjoying his handling of the poetic medium to such an extent that he plays tricks with it. When Dipsychus breaks for a time into hexameters, the Spirit amuses himself in a parenthesis: "(Hexameters, by all that's odious,/Beshod with rhyme to run melodious!)" (240). The Spirit's reference to Byron at the beginning of Scene V recalls that poet's outrageous couplets: "The ground which Byron used to ride on/And do I don't know what beside on."

Clough also calls up at least one echo for a more significant purpose: in Dipsychus's long speech on indecisiveness in Scene IX, the echoes of Hamlet's soliloquies on the same theme underscore Dipsychus's debate with himself. It is subtly done, the accent and phrasing near enough to suggest Shakespeare's, but far enough away to avoid wholly humorous parody.

> O me, when the great deed e'en now has broke
> Like a man's hand the horizon's level line,

> So soon to fill the zenith with rich clouds;
> Oh, in this narrow interspace, this moment,
> This list and selvage of a glorious time,
> To despair of the great and sell to the mean!
> O thou of little faith, what hast thou done?
> Yet if the occasion coming should find *us*
> Undexterous, incapable? In light things
> Prove thou the arms thou long'st to glorify,
> Nor fear to work up from the lowest ranks
> Whence come great Nature's captains. And high deeds
> Haunt not the fringy edges of the fight,
> But the pell-mell of men. Oh, what and if
> E'en now by lingering here I let them slip,
> Like an unpractised spyer through a glass,
> Still pointing to the blank, too high! And yet,
> In dead details to smother vital ends
> Which should give life to them; in the deft trick
> Of prentice-handling to forget great art,
> To base mechanical adroitness yield
> The Inspiration and the Hope, a slave!
>
> (271)

As a final example of Clough's control, one should look at his handling of the vowel sounds in Dipsychus's well-known dream and note the modulation from the happy "ting, ting" to the dolorous "dong, dong" as the bell ringing in his head first tinkles a joyful response to the news that there is no God and then tolls a sad second thought.

There are in *Dipsychus,* of course, a number of debts to Goethe's version of the Faust legend. Clough's painting of Venice recalls passages from the section entitled "Before the City Gate" (Vor den Tor) in the first part of *Faust:*

> Out of the hollow gloomy gate
> Surges and scatters a motley horde.
> All seek sunshine. They celebrate
> The resurrection of the Lord.
> They celebrate the resurrection of the Lord.
> For they themselves are resurrected
> From lowly houses, musty as stables,
> From trades to which they are subjected,
> From the pressures of roofs and gables,
> From the stifling and narrow alleys,

From the church's reverent night
They have emerged into the light.[7]

The Spirit's song in Part Two of *Dipsychus* bears some affinities with the peasant's song in the same section, and it is perhaps not too much to see a resemblance between the sharp quatrains of Goethe's Walpurgis Night's Dream (Walpurgisnachtsraum) and the well-known lines of Dipsychus's dream in Scene V. Similarities in the substance of speeches by Faust and Dipsychus, Mephistopheles and the Spirit could undoubtedly be pointed out. But, after all, the differences in tone, scope, and structure are immense; and it is impossible to believe that Clough could have deceived himself into believing that he was in any way competing with Goethe. Instead, he was probably counting on the obvious differences between the grandeur and sweep of Goethe's treatment and the circumscribed limits of the conflict in Dipsychus's mind to convey an ironical depreciation of the significance of Dipsychus's struggle.

CHAPTER 6

Resolution and Acceptance: The Shorter Poems after 1849

THE Oxford edition of Clough's poetry prints a total of eighty-six poems in the sections titled "Shorter Poems" and "Unfinished Poems." With the exception of the eight which were probably written during the same years as the poems published in *Ambarvalia*, most and perhaps all were written in the years 1849–53.[1] For many, any more exact dating must remain conjectural; but to regard all but the eight as the product of the four and a half years which fall between the publication of *Ambarvalia* and Clough's virtual abandonment of poetry on his return to England is to err but little.

With the obvious exceptions of "The Latest Decalogue" and "Say Not the Struggle," these poems have not received the attention they merit. The dozen or so written after Clough's departure for America to express his longing for Blanche and England are fairly conventional and will not be discussed. But almost all the others are interesting in content, execution, or both. Most important, despite having been written during the same period that Clough was at work on *Amours* and *Dipsychus,* many of the most striking and ambitious poems present the grounds for a hopefulness altogether absent from the main characters of those two poems.

I *Clough's Resolution*

As I read the poems of these years, they express Clough's final abandonment of the long wait for a special insight, and his formulation of the position that not only is it unprofitable to make action await such insight, but also it is necessary to act if man is to gain knowledge and understanding. Mrs. Clough's "Memoir" describes Clough's acceptance of the post at the Education Office and subsequent marriage as the beginning of true happiness and contentment.[2] It has been fashionable to assume that his wife, mistaking acquiescence for fulfillment and overlooking his virtual abandonment of poetry during these years, has not unnaturally exaggerated Clough's peace and tranquillity. There is no reason, however, to doubt that Clough was indeed a great deal happier than he had been for many years, and little evidence that Clough much missed poetry or would have developed his talents in new directions. He had used poetry largely as an intellectual tool; there was no longer any task for it to do. His wife is also quite right, it seems to me, in taking his return to England and marriage as the date when the last obstacles to his happiness were removed.

On the other hand, what Mrs. Clough failed to recognize is that, prior to the settling of the outer details of Clough's life, an inner resolution had to be reached. This resolution, which dates from before the return from America, Clough worked out for himself. Within a few months of his arrival in the United States, Clough's letters reveal an abatement of the inner conflicts which had absorbed the greater portion of his intellectual life since early in his Oxford career. He writes to Blanche in January, 1853, that he is "a good deal changed . . . from what I was in England, and I don't think on the whole you would be troubled much with my old habits of doubting, etc., etc." [3] And in February he writes: "Turn the thing over as we will we can't *make* sure—but doubt as we will about things in particular, we can for the whole *feel* sure." [4] By April, Palgrave was writing to Clough that he and Frederick Temple were "much rejoiced" at the happier tone of recent letters from Clough.[5] Clough's letters do not suddenly become joyous; his practical economic difficulties were too great for that. But, despite a tone of querulousness which often intrudes when he writes of the practical problems of making a living, there is little hint that he is much plagued by doubts as to what he can believe.

The outlines of Clough's resolution are to be found among the poems of 1849–52, although on first examination these seem simply to carry on the old debates. "Say not the struggle," Clough's most positive affirmation, is partially balanced by "Bethesda. A Sequel." The former, with its hopeful belief that

> For while the tired waves, vainly breaking,
> Seem here no painful inch to gain,

> Far back through creeks and inlets making
> Come, silent, flooding in, the main,

is, after all, only the most fortunately phrased of Clough's statements of his belief in fighting the good fight. The problems of
what to fight for and how to identify friend and foe, already raised
in the *Bothie* and in some of the poems of *Ambarvalia*, are posed
in "Bethesda," a sequel to, or more exactly, a palinode to the first
of Clough's poems in *Ambarvalia*, "The human spirits saw I on a
day." In the sequel, the spirit previously commended for his commitment to duty is found among the other sick and maimed waiting by the pool of Bethesda to be cured. The spirit is still devoted
to duty but is unable to distinguish the demands of duty from the
common demands of the world; he concludes, "'I know not, I
must do as other men are doing.'" The poet is unable to know
whether either the pool, whatever its power, or Christ will heal
him.

"Easter Day" and "Easter Day II" clash directly. The first is
probably Clough's most complete denial of the grounds of religious faith, and certainly one of his most technically effective
poems. Denying and rationalizing away all the accounts of the
miracles of Christ's resurrection, Clough returns again and again
to the conclusion that "He is not risen, no,/He lies and moulders
low,/Christ is not risen." Nor does the poet find it possible to base
a faith or code upon Christ's message, as does Matthew Arnold in
"The Better Part" or as Clough himself had in a letter to his sister.[6] However, "Easter Day II" denies the previous conclusion.

> Though He be dead, He is not dead.
> In the true Creed
> He is yet risen indeed,
> Christ is yet risen.

But this poem never attains the force of expression of the first
part; nor, though it suggests a shifting of the grounds of argument
in the phrase "In the true Creed," ever announces that creed.

Nevertheless, in spite of these opposing pairs, a group of poems
from the period reveals a new strain in Clough's thought and a
movement toward a thoughtful acceptance of the order of things
which, if not certainly optimistic, is not the result of despair.

These are the poems exploring the biblical incidents which seem
to have most fascinated Clough: the story of Jacob, Leah, and
Rachel; the Fall; and Cain's murder of Abel. Clough's sense of
the significance of these stories and of the importance of interpreting them aright appears in a paragraph from his "Notes on the
Religious Tradition" in the midst of his statement of things which
"are conceivable" or "may be true" (which he provisionally accepts on faith):

> It may be true that Man has fallen, though Adam and Eve are
> legendary. It may be a divine fact that God is a Person, and not a
> sort of Natural Force—and it may have happened that the tales of
> his personal appearance to Abraham[,] Isaac[,] and Jacob were the
> means of sustaining, and conveying down to posterity that belief—and
> yet that he never sat in the tent on the plains of Mamre, nor wrestled
> with Jacob by night; nor spoke with Moses in the Mount.—[7]

The Jacob story is alluded to a number of times in the *Bothie*,
where its significance has to do with the combination of the earthy
and spiritual in marriage and with the truth that the higher values
and meaning of marriage are produced by laboring in the vine-
yard, not by mere aspiration. Clough returns to the story in "Jacob's Wives," a long dialogue in which Leah and Rachel each
claims the prime place in Jacob's affections: Leah pleading her
four sons; Rachel the strong love which she had from the first
inspired in Jacob. The poem merits closer study than it has received. Its mood, despite the wrangling of the two wives, is never
shrill; and it ends in a tranquil scene suggesting a sense of almost
mystic comfort:

> These are the words of Jacob's wives, who sat
> In the tent door, and listened to their speech,
> The spring beside him, and above the palm,
> While all the sheep were gathered for the night.

The situation, as Clough develops it, symbolizes in the wives the
continuing struggle between two goals, both good in their way,
and in the figure of Jacob, listening but not taking part and seemingly calmed by the natural scene, the man who recognizes the
irreconcilable and the irresolvable in the world but accepts in life
whatever happiness and understanding he can attain. The tech-

nique used in the poem is both less explicit and wider in its range of meanings than any Clough had previously employed. The fruit of marriage with Leah had appeared without delay, that of marriage with Rachel must still await God's grace and thus is a natural symbol for the direct communication with God still aspired to; but beyond this the opposition is susceptible to innumerable other interpretations.

This reading of "Jacob's Wives" is supported by the "Jacob" poem which immediately follows it in the Oxford edition, though probably written at least a year later. In this monologue Jacob recounts his struggles both with men and God. Not like Isaac or Abraham's has been his life: "They communed, Israel wrestled with the Lord." Nevertheless, though unsatisfied and glad that his life is over, Jacob can bless God and feel that that life "was a work appointed me of thee." Even more important is his recognition and acceptance of "The chase, the competition, and the craft/Which seem to be the poison of our life/And yet is the condition of our life!" It is a mystery why man's imperfect and sometimes seemingly blind participation in the world has been ordained; one can either vex and wear out one's spirit attempting to see behind the mystery, or one can accept both its existence and impenetrability. The latter is Jacob's choice—and his acceptance is presented with no hint of the mocking irony Clough is so quick to direct against what he regards as facile solutions.

The same thought about the necessity of those desires and drives which force one "To wear out heart and nerves and brain" is worked out in a short poem from one of Clough's 1851 notebooks of which the quoted line is the opening. Man knows better than to "Be eager, angry, fierce, and hot"; but the poet's conclusion is the same expressed by Jacob:

> It is not in itself a bliss
> To combat and contrive,
> Only it is precisely this
> That keeps us all alive.

The expression of a faith grounded in a trusting acquiescence in the mixed good and evil of life recurs again in "The Song of Lamech," conjecturally dated by Clough himself from February, 1849. The passage in Genesis (IV: 23–24) known as "The Song of

Lamech" has been interpreted in a variety of ways; the most usual explanation considers the passage as a song in which Lamech boasts of his custom of taking vengeance for injuries. The reference to Cain in the passage has generally been regarded as acknowledging the genealogy which makes Lamech a descendant of Cain rather than of Seth. Clough's treatment, however, interprets the song as Lamech's faith in God's mercy which, as he relates, was shown even to Cain, his (implied) ancestor. Clough thus takes the passage "for I have slain a man to my wounding, and a young man to my hurt" not as a boast that Lamech will kill a man who wounds him but as meaning that, in killing another, a man wounds himself (an interpretation for which Clough could have found warrant in some of the old Jewish commentators [8]). Thus the poem, after retelling the story of Cain's exile to the land of Nod and adding Adam's vision of Cain's reconciliation to Abel and God, ends with Lamech's expectation of God's mercy:

> Though to his wounding did he slay a man,
> Yea, and a young man to his hurt he slew,
> Fear not ye wives nor sons of Lamech fear:
> If unto Cain was safety given and rest,
> Shall Lamech surely and his people die?

In addition to the apocryphal reconciliation, two points are significant about the version of the Cain story that Clough has Lamech tell. The first is that, up to the moment of his death, Cain sees alternate visions of good and evil; any final assurance that all is well is withheld from this life. The second is Cain's comparison of his own exile with that of Adam and Eve from Eden, which, one must remember, is, paradox of paradoxes, the "fortunate fall." The murder of Abel was ordained by God for his own purposes.

II *"The Mystery of the Fall"*

This interpretation of the problem of evil as resolved in the "paradox of the fortunate fall" is further developed in the most interesting of Clough's shorter poems, "The Mystery of the Fall." This ambitious poem goes beyond any of the attempts to formulate a comprehensive view of life to be found elsewhere in Clough's poetry. Put together by his editors from scenes found in four notebooks and one folder, and manifestly unfinished, the reconstructed poem has, as both Mrs. Clough and the Oxford editors have commented, a surprising coherence.

The first scene opens the morning after the Fall, as Adam, with a frankness most un-Victorian, sums up the sequence of feelings associated with the sexual act: "One, two, and three, and four,— the appetite,/ The enjoyment, the aftervoid, the thinking of it—" Adam feels no despair at the fall; he is ready to begin the work which is to be man's punishment. Eve, however, expresses a fifth feeling: guilt. Adam's answer is that the fall and the exile from Eden were necessary to growth, an answer which Dipsychus also proposed:[9] "That which we were, we could no more remain/Than in the moist provocative vernal mould/A seed its suckers close, and rest a seed"(410).

From the ensuing dialogue it appears that no angel with a flaming sword but Eve's conviction of their guilt and unworthiness to remain had driven the two from Eden. Adam tries to explain Eve's fears "Of the serpent, and the apple, and the curse" as a dream engendered by "the first maternity of Man," but he is unable to convince her. She brings him to admit that at times he has heard a voice which brought panic, though he insists that more often the voice he hears warns "On! On! it is the folly of the child/To choose his path and straightway think it wrong,/And turn right back, or lie on the ground to weep"(413).

In Scene II, Adam, now alone, reveals that he himself is seized at moments with a sense of guilt; but at other times he finds himself calmly trying to analyze the meaning of all his experiences, including his dark thoughts of guilt. Though he believes that all could be understood were there more time, he knows that work must be done, and he gives up the problem to begin his duties.

Ambivalences run through the entire poem. Eve is at times too sanguine, at times too despondent; Cain exults in having killed Abel but nevertheless feels his sin strongly. Even Abel, the pious brother, has moments when he doubts his own motives. However, these ambivalences do not create a mere fruitless and never-ending debate; instead, they produce the sense that the meaning of life and of such words as "guilt" and "sin" and even "goodness" are indeed a mystery and will remain so. Clough's Adam and Eve employ quite sophisticated theological concepts for beings who have so newly begun to vex themselves with religious controversy. It is likely that such anachronisms as their implied familiarity with the doctrine of the elect is intended to remind the reader that all theological systems take their rise in the attempt to solve the eternal enigmas that would have suggested themselves even to the first man and woman.

Cain's statement to Adam, "You read the earthly as my mother heaven" implies that no one reads both. But, though these mysteries cannot be solved, certain principles of life are stated in the last two scenes with neither implicit nor explicit qualification. Cain declares that he must not forget his brother's murder. He is what he is, has done what he has done; but in his sinful state he finds it good to welcome work: "To toil the livelong day, and at the end,/Instead of rest, re-carve into my brow/The dire memorial mark of what still is" (431). Work remains, as for Adam, the punishment for, but also the release from, an action which seems absolutely wrong and absolutely fated. To worship as Abel had done by turning his eyes to heaven would be for Cain the worst of sins; work is to be his form of worship.

Clough's belief that setting one's hand to useful work is the one thing needful, comprising most of the duties of this life and representing the most fitting form of worship, may be traced from his Rugby days through the *Bothie* and "Qui Laborat, Orat" to its expression in the "Mystery of the Fall" in its deepest and most intense form. His most interesting prose statement of this reverence for work, which had its roots in the teachings of Dr. Arnold and Carlyle, appears in his University College lecture on Wordsworth. Turning aside to comment on Walter Scott, Clough describes Scott's enjoyment of the baronial life at Abbotsford as disappointing, but as making one "really thankful, while we read, for the foreknowledge that so strong and capable a soul was ere the end to have some nobler work allotted it, if not in the way of action, at any rate in that of endurance." [10] This is perhaps a somewhat uncharitable evaluation; but such a comment on the uses of adversity is entirely consistent with Clough's serious view of life and one which is, after all, quite orthodox within the Christian tradition.

Adam's reply to Cain looks forward to comfort and consolation in knowledge—a knowledge, however, of "the certainty of things," not insight into the mystery. That is, man's knowledge can extend only to a recognition of the constant forms in which the mystery manifests itself. Finally, in the last scene, Adam's vision corresponds to that in "The Song of Lamech" in its portrayal of Abel's forgiveness of Cain and the death of all—Adam, Eve, Cain, Abel—as the prelude to something hopeful but unknown. Adam, after admitting all the agony of his life and the lack of any sure guidance "Except a kind of impetus within," is able to say:

> Yet, in despite of much, in lack of more,
> Life has been beautiful to me my son,
> And if they call me, I will come again.
> But sleep is sweet, and I would sleep, my son.
> Behold, the words of Adam have an end.
>
> (434)

Adam, who is to be numbered among Clough's other "divided" souls, has reached this acceptance of the necessary imperfection of life by giving up his fruitless attempts to pierce the life's mysteries in favor of work and action.

Evident in these poems, and especially in the "Song of Lamech" and in "The Mystery of the Fall," is a resolution of the religious questioning which had filled so much of Clough's poetry. It is equally obvious that the resolution was not achieved through the construction of a philosophical system nor through the adoption of any new creed. To some extent, of course, the sense of acceptance in the biblical poems is to be found in the whole mood of the Pentateuch, which sets forth history as a process ordained by God for purposes unfathomable to man. But very likely Clough chose to use biblical incidents as vehicles to express his new attitude toward experience precisely because this interpretation of history already lay behind them. Nor is the atmosphere of these poems strictly biblical: Clough has not hesitated to alter both the details and to some extent the spirit of these stories, and the effect which they produce, especially in the emphasis on the mystery which lies behind the fates of individuals, is rather like that of the Greek tragedies Clough knew so well.

The care with which the mention of any attribute of the Deity is avoided in Clough's handling of the biblical stories (which helps to produce the sense of mystery of human destiny) presents the much less specific concept of Deity which remained after scientific discovery and the Higher Criticism had pared away attri-

bute after attribute. Clough is at this point closer to Matthew
Arnold's definition of God as the "Eternal, not ourselves, that
makes for righteousness" than either he or Arnold would perhaps have been aware of. There is also an echo of Goethe in the
argument that the evil of the present may be the ground of the
good of the future—though this doctrine in its "felix culpa" form
need not have been taken directly from Goethe but from a long
tradition which has found recent expression in Sartre's "The Flies"
and MacLeish's *J. B.*

III *The "Seven Sonnets"*

One other very interesting work from this time is the group of
sonnets from Clough's 1851 (A) notebook. First brought together
in the 1867 edition as "Seven Sonnets on the Thought of Death,"
the seven mutually qualify one another; each tentative position
questions the others. Clough had elsewhere raised all the questions and stated all the positions presented in the "Seven Sonnets,"
which is perhaps the reason he never gave them a final revision
and excluded them from the poems forwarded to Norton for the
projected American edition. The issues they raise had been debated in his earlier poems, and, by the end of the 1849–52 period,
they had been transcended. Nevertheless, Clough erred in his
judgment about the importance of these poems, for they are technically among the best poems he ever wrote. He achieved in them
an economy and an intensity which he never surpassed. Though
the order in which they were to appear is not absolutely clear, and
may not have finally been determined by Clough, the sequence
established by Mrs. Clough seems probable. The general scheme
is in any case apparent.[11]

In the first sonnet the questions of the meaning of life and of
whether one dares hope that there is a larger, invisible plan arise
out of the contemplation of the death of a person "whose sole
office was to exist." The second sonnet cites man's highest aspira-
tions as grounds for believing that there is much more to the cycle
of human existence than the span from birth to death. The third,
of which the last three lines are conjectural, seems to be building
toward an affirmation; but the fourth, in reaction, asks if the "in-
ward strong assurance" may not be the result of an illusion. The
fifth alludes to former hopes now "dead-slumbering," presumably
a specific allusion to the growing doubt and skepticism of the time

—Arnold's receding "sea of faith"—and asks how many ages must pass before time reconstructs "The skiey picture we had gazed upon." The sixth argues for the bare hope that there is another existence after death; and the last, recognizing that the previous sonnet had been too tentative, takes what seems the most irrefutable fact, man's certainty of his own existence, as the ground for hope: "And always 'tis a fact that we are here;/And with being here, doth palsy-giving fear,/Whoe'er can ask, or hope accord the best?"

The whole range of inconclusive speculation which comprises so much of Clough's work is compressed here into seven sonnets, the tautness of expression necessary to that compression adding an unusual intensity and bringing forth a more imaginative treatment than Clough generally achieved. Sonnet V is a good example of these qualities:

> If it is thou whose casual hand withdraws
> What it at first as casually did make,
> Say what amount of ages it will take
> With tardy rare occurrences of laws,
> And subtle multiplicities of cause,
> The thing they once had made us to remake;
> May hopes dead-slumbering dare to reawake,
> E'en after utmost interval of pause?
> What revolutions must have passed, before
> The great celestial cycles shall restore
> The starry [sign] whose present hour is gone;
> What worse than dubious chances interpose,
> With cloud and sunny gleam to recompose
> The skiey picture we had gazed upon.

On the other hand, the colloquial tone which Clough so much desired is for once maintained without awkwardness. Simple diction is invested with a rhetorical power which at times reminds one of Emily Dickinson:

> That when a certain period has passed by
> People of genius and of faculty,
> Leaving behind them some result to show,
> Having performed some function, should forego
> A task which younger hands can better ply,
> Appears entirely natural.

But the comparison with Dickinson recalls to mind Clough's characteristic weakness—the absence of imagery. Even here, in some of the best of Clough's work, the reader is disappointed in the expectation of a flash of imagery which will illuminate the abstract statement. However, this weakness is partially offset by the interest generated through Clough's careful tracing of the odd movements of the human mind. In reading the first sonnet, for instance, one feels at first inclined to object that the deaths of neither children nor those who have been unusually productive strike one as appearing "entirely natural." But one sees by the end of the sonnet the accuracy of Clough's observation: we all realize that childhood and innocence and genius are not proof against death; thus, in one sense at least, we accept their destruction. On the other hand, we are reminded that those lives which appear to be outside time, because nothing is expected of them, do seem in an odd way as though they should be invulnerable. A similar psychological reaction is outlined in Sonnet III, in which Clough examines how it is that the contemplation of death itself may create hope.

IV   *The Review of* The Soul

The most direct evidence we have of what Clough was thinking at this time is found in his review of F. W. Newman's *The Soul*. The circumstances of the composition of this "review" are unknown; no publication has been discovered prior to the 1869 edition. It was, however, certainly written during the same four years as the poems under present discussion: an early draft is to be found in Clough's 1850 (Venice) notebook. There are at least three passages in this largely favorable review which are of importance for interpreting Clough's religious position at this time.

The most striking passage is the reference, halfway through the essay, to his personal experience. In speaking of a desire for a "sensible consciousness" of God or a "recognition of the sensuous presence" of Jesus or Mary, Clough states: "To believe such spiritual communion possible is perhaps not unwise; to expect it is perilous; to seek it pernicious.—To make it our business here is simply suicidal; to indulge in practices with a view to it most unwholesome and dangerous." After developing the metaphor of spiritual disease, which Newman had already used, Clough continues: "Is this vague and unmeaning declamation[?] Ah, reader,

it is not pleasant for the new convalescent to talk of his sick-room
phenomena, to re-enter the diseased past, and dwell again among
details of pathology and morbid anatomy." [12]

We have here Clough's violent renunciation of his past religious
attitude insofar as he had expected a vision of truth or the discovery of signposts for his personal guidance. Moreover, although
containing no other direct references to Clough's own experiences,
the essay carries throughout the personal tone of a man speaking
from the basis of his own hard-won principles. In later raising the
question of *how* one was to put into practice the desire to serve
God which arises out of "religious exercises and devotional indul-
gence" and in suggesting that the attempt to do God's Will very
often ends with "the river of piety" losing itself "in the sands of
the World," Clough is clearly speaking from his own experience of
the incommensurability of the ideal and the actual. The desire for
a sense of personal relationship with God is for Clough the root of
spiritual pathology. In place of all the rituals and duties designed
to achieve such a state, Clough substitutes a few very modest
principles.

His first principle is the same one he praises in Newman: "Believe thine own soul." One's faith can be guaranteed neither by
historical facts, "however strongly attested," nor by theological articles, "however ancient and venerable." Faith must be grounded
in an inner conviction common to most men. Clough's position on
this point is very much like that he had described as belonging to
the eighteenth century:

Morality survives, we know not well how, in Hume. Religion appears to be driven to its inmost lines of defenses, to be fighting from
its enceincture of fortification, in Butler's Analogical argument. And
Johnson, in the last resort can but confute Hume, as Berkeley, with
a stamp upon the ground. . . .

. . . How different from the idea of a religion meeting all the
otherwise disappointed hopes, fulfilling all the profoundest and most
secret needs of our spiritual nature is the great argument of the Analogy, which nakedly stated would seem to run, that we have no right
to claim a religion according to our own fancies, that as the world
of ordinary facts is full of difficulties, so also it is to be expected, will
be religion also. How matter of fact, and as good people would say
—how low, is the morality of Johnson; how indiscriminate moreover
he is obliged in his extreme need to be in his religious faith, and de-

votional observances. Nevertheless—there is a cogency in this resting
upon only the lowest grounds. The winter-vitality of the moral convictions of Hume is worth more than any summery exuberance of
sentiment: Butler's argument does hold water: Johnson's character
does prove something.[13]

One's hope and faith must be grounded finally, as is Adam's, in "a
kind of impetus within, whose sole credentials were that trust itself."

The second principle is that the individual's conscience should
not be so overdeveloped, either by his training or by his own
straining after righteousness, that all deviation from a moral code
seems sin. "One could almost fancy that in the spiritual, as in the
intellectual region, there are *Antinomies*. It is needful to believe
that between the doing and not doing of a given act there is a
difference simply infinite—it is needful also to believe that it is
indifferent." [14] From his discussion of this point, it becomes clear
that Clough is especially finding fault with the belief that it is
sinful to take action in a matter about which the individual has
no absolute moral certainty. But he also insists on the damage
that is done to a child who is made to feel that each error he
makes is a sin. A portion of Dr. Arnold's method is here rejected
explicitly on the same grounds that the "uncle" attacks it in the
epilogue to *Dipsychus*.

The third principle is that one must look at the world around
him as well as into his soul to determine what it is he is to do. "We
have said, Look not up into the empty airs, but upon the solid,
somewhat dirty earth around underfoot." [15] When Clough argues
in "Notes on the Religious Tradition" that that tradition—which
he defines as the substance of what it is essential to believe and to
do—is found "everywhere," he is insisting that man look not only
up to heaven and within himself but out into the world and down
at the common dirt in which he works. Men are all, in a sense,
like Cain after the murder of Abel—not pure enough to look
up to heaven; but they are nevertheless capable of worshipping
and of finding some meaning through recognizing facts and wel-
coming work.

There is a touch, however, of Clough's inconclusiveness and ten-
tativeness even in the review, his firmest statement of religious
belief. As he admits in the essay, he has hardly given any direct

advice about what the individual is to do to enter that Kingdom of Heaven which Clough finds without as well as within man. But the principle of believing one's own soul would seem to be offered as the ground for a faith that there is a God; the principle of not refusing to act simply out of fear of doing the wrong thing argues for the importance of trying *actively* to serve that God; and the principle of looking out into the world around implies that one will necessarily find that which needs doing. These principles, then, form a religion which actively reforms and improves the order of society while denying that the performance of religious exercises in any way serves God.

V *Hopeful Acceptance*

That Clough had, in these years, won his way to a set of principles upon which he was prepared to take his stand is apparent from a number of other poems of this time. Even "Sa Majesté très Chrétienne," which some readers have found dark and despairing, is essentially a statement of the position found in the review of Newman's book. The poem opens with the King's admission to his confessor of a troubled mind and spirit and with expression of his wish that he could have remained an innocent child, an acolyte. One should recall that one of the traditional interpretations of the story of the Fall is that man was intended to remain in Eden, living within the limits of understanding and action appropriate to a child. The King's "I would I were, as God intended me,/A little quiet harmless acolyte" thus acquires considerable irony in the light of Clough's conviction (as expressed in "Lamech" and "The Mystery of the Fall") that God had *not* intended such a state to continue, that man had to become responsible.

It is the combination of responsibility, uncertainty, and never-conquered "bad prickings of the animal heats" that the King complains of—the difficulty of human decision-making multiplied by his position as ruler. Yet, like Clough's Adam, the King, though admitting error and sin, closes his statement to the confessor without despair, even with a kind of accepting faith:

> Depraved, that is, degraded am I—Sins
> Which yet I see not how I should have shunned,
> Have, in despite of all the means of grace,
> Submission perfect to the appointed creed,

> And absolution-plenary and prayers,
> Possessed me, held, and changed—yet after all
> Somehow I think my heart within is pure.
>
> (72)

In *Ambarvalia* Clough's general approach is to devote one poem to one point of view, one to another; and *Amours* and *Dipsychus* are each based on the tensions which lead to the defeat of the individual who is torn between conflicting points of view. The most significant of the shorter poems dating from 1849–52 interpret such conflicts as mysteries which must be recognized but need not, in fact cannot, be resolved by man. That is, man finds himself unable to construct a system which will assure him exactly what he is to believe and how he is to act; but, when he realizes that he is not required to reconcile all anomalies or to choose once for all between conflicting concepts, his mind ceases to be a battlefield. He can then continue to speculate and to try to understand problems about which he entertains several alternative answers; but, if he recognizes that he may make choices and take actions without having first "solved" all problems, that it is not necessary that everything wait on the attainment of a whole and consistent world-view, he is freed to act and live. The opposed views and conflicting moods represented by Clough's Adam, Eve, Cain, and Jacob are recognized as eternally existing.

Though poems of a darker cast are sprinkled among those which can be assigned to these years, the majority either pick up one of the hopeful views of life already traced or express a kind of general faith and hopefulness. The poem beginning "In controversial foul impureness" counsels "in faith and inner sureness/ Possess thy soul and let it be," and it develops in the fifth and sixth stanzas a variant of the image of the great flow of the sea or stream from "Say not the struggle." "Whence are ye, vague desires" expresses the faith, inexplicable but sure, that, despite the pain and misery brought about by man's unruly desires, these desires were "For some good end designed/for man and womankind." With this concept may be contrasted Dipsychus's cry that all might be well were it not for "This interfering, enslaving, o'ermastering demon of craving." [16]

There are so many short poems that an attempt to discuss them could be nothing more than a long, repetitious catalogue. The reader who works through them with attention to the total theme of each (rather than to individual lines which can be incorporated in a biographical explanation of Clough's "failure") can hardly help feeling that the balance has swung away from the old, vexed, constantly problematic views of the world. Other poems to be especially noted are "The grasses green of sweet content," the last two stanzas of which are an unqualified affirmation of the order of things so tentatively accepted by Philip in lines fifty-five and fifty-six of Section IX of the *Bothie;* "Even the Winds and the Sea Obey," which describes the overcoming of obstacles by the will (another way of saying that action brings about that which mere contemplation would pronounce impossible); and "To spend uncounted years," which ironically asks if constantly to debate "the problem of our being here," while withholding a conclusion until more evidence is in, is "the object, end and law,/And purpose of our being here."

Of significance also are the happy lyrics, "Les Vaches" and "July's Farewell." Technically among the best poems Clough ever wrote, these, unlike the vast bulk of his poetry, seem to have been composed for the pure joy of writing verses. The first has certain Classical echoes, and the second is intended to suggest, but not entirely imitate, Burns and the Scottish lyric. They must be counted as part of the evidence of the lightheartedness which Clough felt at this time. Finally, the effectiveness of the well-known "The Latest Decalogue" depends not only on the sharpness but the breadth of humor of the satire.[17]

The theme of the importance and necessity of work, which runs through the poems of this period, reiterates the conclusions of the *Bothie;* but, at the same time, it goes far beyond the earlier poem in considering the significance of work. It has become for Clough a form of worship and a means of finding truth. Even when it seems to lead men to sin, it may be God's instrument for accomplishing purposes beyond man's understanding.

In the review "Recent English Poetry" Clough had called for a more hopeful and inspiriting literature than England was then producing. "Cannot the Divine Song in some way indicate to us our unity, though from a great way off, with those happier things; inform us, and prove to us, that though we are what we are, we may yet, in some way, even in our abasement, even by and through our daily work, be related to the purer existence."[18]

Clough had by the beginning of 1853 achieved for himself such a faith and had given it subdued expression in "Jacob," "The Mystery of the Fall," and "Sa Majesté très Chrétienne"; but beyond that he declined to attempt the bold and triumphant Divine Song for which he had called.

Clough was now ready to abandon speculation and its poetic exploration for work, but ironically he seems to have been so exhausted by years of intellectual turmoil and so overwhelmed by the difficulty of earning enough to support Blanche that he was unable to make purely practical decisions. Once in America, he could not decide whether to stay and try to earn a living as a teacher or to return to England and take the position offered in the Education Office. There is no evidence that any other intellectual scruples were behind his indecision at this time, but much that he was simply unable to decide on the course most likely to make his marriage possible within a reasonable time.

In resolving his intellectual perplexities, Clough did not abandon the rigor of his own thought. That he remained very much concerned about religious beliefs and that he still felt it necessary to resist all beliefs he could not accept are made clear by his correspondence with J. C. Shairp in 1853 in which Shairp pleads: "Nothing you can say will make me change my holdings; but I wish not to quarrel with you and therefore beg that you will write no more on these subjects," and a month later, "Please, No more of this!" [19] Indeed, perhaps the great source of unhappiness Clough had in these later years was his sense of alienation from his old friends. Holding to the bare essentials of theistic belief, content to accept all beyond as mystery, and feeling that dogmatic statements about anything beyond those essentials was folly, it is no wonder that in 1853 Clough wrote to Blanche: "Somehow or other all those friendships seem to be going off rather. They have all got so *churchy;* there is no possibility of getting on thoroughly—Matt Arnold is not churchy—though his wife is, which is a pity." [20]

This discussion may perhaps not unsuitably be brought to a conclusion by mentioning two anachronistic parallels, that of French secular existentialism, which denies the possibility of finding any certain guide for action, yet urges the necessity of committing oneself to action and of taking responsibility for it (as do Clough's Adam and Cain), and that of Kierkegaardian Christian existentialism which emphasizes the paradoxes of man's experience and the impossibility of rationally analyzing the purposes or even existence of God. The danger of making too much of such parallels is obvious—far too many attempts have been made to use existentialism as a key to unlock "deeper" meanings in writers who are alleged to have been ur-existentialists. Clearly Clough's faith is not to be equated with Sartre's denial of the existence of God, and Kierkegaard's method of guaranteeing the validity of Christian faith by its "absurdity" would hardly have appealed to Clough. But the parallels do point out why Clough seems so congenial to twentieth-century thought, as well as why his position seemed so negative in the nineteenth century when, however much challenged, the orthodox theological position still dominated religious thought.

CHAPTER 7

Explicit Statements of Belief:
Clough's Prose

A S ALREADY stated, there is reason to regard Clough as one who wrote poetry as a way of giving vent to his own internal debates and of trying out various viewpoints; he hoped perhaps that those doctrines to which he could poetically give the most convincing ring of truth might well be nearest the truth. He seems also to have enjoyed indulging in poetic exercises, returning again and again to attempts at putting the *Iliad* in English hexameters and now and then trying to catch the tone of some earlier English poet. But there is little evidence, in either his poetry, prose essays, or letters, that he gave much thought to the techniques of poetry, or that he attempted to work out a poetic theory to govern his own writing.[1]

I *Clough's Prose Style*

Since Clough seems never to have wholeheartedly dedicated himself to poetry, several critics have suggested that his true medium should have been prose. Such a judgment finds support in his tendency toward a colloquial, indeed prosy, tone in his poetry and in the readableness of his letters to friends. On the evidence of his letters, Clough might have been a successful essayist had he been able to sharpen his epistolary style and otherwise modify it to the uses of the essay, but the essays he has left indicate that he was never able to do this. His most readable prose is found in the lectures on poetry delivered at London University, but there is nothing about these to make them memorable. When he tried to achieve a more personal and effective style, as in his two most serious essays, those on the Oxford Retrenchment Association and Newman's *The Soul,* or as in his light and jaunty letters of Parepidemus, the style becomes exaggerated.

The whole tone and style of his serious essays is that of a preacher delivering rhetorically wrapped wisdom from the eminence of the pulpit. His Rugby essays are almost embarrassingly earnest, though this quality is easily attributable to his having acquired quite an impressive mastery of syntax and vocabulary before he had anything much to say. The schoolboy who learns the rhetorical devices before he has the maturity to have anything to pour into these forms is bound to sound as pretentious as Clough does in his treatment of Macaulay's "Battle of Ivry": " 'The Battle of Ivry'!—I remember well when I first read it, and how strong was the impression it made upon me; this indeed, I cannot forget, for the lapse of two years has not effaced, or even dulled it." [2]

But, having acquired a mechanical facility with language rather early, he failed to develop a personal style or to learn quite how to adjust tone and style to his subject. His undergraduate essays show little advance over those contributed to the *Rugby Magazine;* in fact, they show a diminishing of the enthusiasm which is the chief charm of the earlier efforts. One should not attempt to make too much of these undergraduate essays—they are merely exercises never intended for publication—but the ease with which Clough turns out conventional treatments of such topics as the moral effect of literature without ever giving flesh and bone to his abstract moralizing bodes ill for a future prose writer. In his prose Clough never quite got over the tendency to float off into cloudy abstractions.

The best example of this failing is probably the essay written in 1847 on the Retrenchment Association at Oxford. The association had been formed by Oxford students to encourage their fellows to reduce expenditures on luxuries and to contribute to the relief of the Irish peasants starving because of the potato famine. The essay, often cited as an example of Clough's social conscience, can as well be cited as reflecting the worst faults of Clough's prose style. Neither the title nor the opening paragraphs make clear where Clough is going to stand. The opening point—a rebuttal of the argument that the association is unnecessary—must be worried out of Clough's prose after careful attention to the references of pronouns in the first paragraphs; and the difficulty of determining Clough's intention is not helped by his serious use of rhetorical devices so heavy that they teeter on the edge of irony or parody.

Clough's consideration of whether a student should request money from his father to give to the relief of the Irish suffers from precisely this fault: ". . . may it not be asked, Is it true that you have not, in point of fact, what comes to the same thing as an allowance? a sum of money which you are expected to call for, beyond which you are expected not to go. . . . The sum which last year the paternal purse would have freely given for ices, will it this year refuse for almsgiving? What with a safe conscience you would have asked for then, will not your conscience suffer you to petition for now?" [3]

Clough is employing rather cumbrous prose artillery on the question of how a student at Oxford should regard his allowance. It is not, of course, that the Irish famine was a small thing but that, after all, the relationship of the Oxford undergraduates to that famine was. In addition, Clough's constant tendency to veer from a significant point to its tangential corollaries leads his reader a merry chase through the consideration of such things as the rights of property and the importance of a privileged and cultured class and then back to no more profound a question than whether an apparent reduction in the usual Oxonian luxuries is not due simply to the unseasonably cold weather. It would be ungracious to devote so much space to making derogatory observations on a minor topical essay by a quite young Oxford tutor were it not that the unsatisfactory nature of such an essay helps to illustrate that poetry was a more congenial medium of expression for Clough.

He himself seems to have realized that his prose was more rhetorical than effective; toward the end of the Oxford Retrenchment essay and also in his review of Newman's *The Soul,* he pauses to protest the importance of what he has been saying, and asks that the issue not be judged on the basis of his heavy rhetoric, admitting in the first work that the circumstances of the college tutor make him highly liable to this defect. At fault in both essays is Clough's tendency to let the seriousness with which he regards a topic overpower his handling of it. His seriousness leads him to employ prose devices which give the effect of pompousness and makes his turning of a question over and over and around and around seem the result of irresolution and disorganization rather than of that free play of the mind at which the essay legitimately aims. Even in the review of *The Soul,* where the subject is serious enough to warrant a searching treatment, Clough falls too much into the patronizing tone of the preacher speaking to his intellectual inferiors to be properly readable. The climactic passage in which Clough asks the reader to report honestly the success of applying religious inspiration to practical life, however much one may agree with its sentiment, has not the tone proper for either the reviewer or the essayist.

The seriousness of Clough's own feeling about the subjects of these two essays cannot be doubted, but he fails to convey his earnestness to the reader. When he attempts to inject a humorous note, the result is the clumsiness of the overserious preacher who tries fumblingly to condescend to his hearer's frailty with an awkward ecclesiastical joke. Indeed, the heavy and oppressive tone of these essays is found elsewhere only in his embarrassingly pious letters to his younger brother and, some seventeen years later, in those lecturing Blanche Smith on the meaning of love, literature, and life.

In the *Letters of Parepidemus* one finds Clough's most pronounced attempt to treat a subject divertingly. Of the six essays in this group—all probably written for periodical publication—only the two actually published in *Putnam's* should be regarded as having received Clough's final revision. The first, "The Evolution of Criteria in Art and Literature," attempts to attract the reader by playing with paradoxical theories about the importance of literature. But the style fails to meet the demands placed on it; it is not light enough to give the effect of the play of mind about a subject. Neither is the second letter, "On Translating Homer," particularly successful in its attempt to combine levity with instruction. Both essays, moreover, end not only with the sense of inconclusiveness which Clough apparently intended but do so awkwardly, without any rounding-off of the subject. In both the serious and lighter essays there are hints of Carlyle's highly figurative style, almost unavoidable perhaps in a mid-nineteenth-century admirer of Carlyle; but Carlyle's sweeping maneuvers were not well adapted to Clough's careful, tentative mode of speculation. Only in letters to Tom Arnold and occasionally J. C. Shairp does he achieve sufficient lightheartedness and distance to use an allusive, metaphorical style with happy effect.

On the other hand, in the brief preface to his *Greek History* assembled from Plutarch and in the *Life of Plutarch*, which prefaces his revisions of the complete *Lives*, where he is dealing only with facts and generally accepted opinions, he employs a subdued style perfectly appropriate to his purposes. In the university lec-

tures, where Clough is primarily concerned with the clear exposi-
tion of literary history, his prose is altogether agreeable. One
wishes that all lecturers could achieve such clarity and organi-
zation and that all were as concerned as Clough that their students see the significant contributions of each literary era. But,
though very good university lectures, these are not significant critical essays.

Despite their formal faults, when regarded simply as documents throwing light on Clough's thought and poetry, the essays
are of considerable interest in their disclosure of the consistency
of Clough's positions. The same points are made, the same views
maintained from essay to essay. In literature, his most frequent
topic is the problem of translation. In economics, it is the necessity
of each man setting his own house in order. In religion, it is the
importance of avoiding all extravagance of belief, observance, or
public statement.

II *The Literary Essays*

Among Clough's literary essays, the contributions to the *Rugby
Magazine* are of little significance beyond establishing his early
preference for Wordsworth and his interest in versification. Those
of his undergraduate years in Oxford are of even less interest since
they do not express ideas he particularly wished to treat at the
time. The first essay dating from after Clough received his bach-
elor's degree, and also the first one published, was "Illustrations
of Latin Lyrical Metres," consisting of a series of his translations,
primarily from Horace, accompanied by brief discussions of the
problems of translation. Of the series of lectures on English literature given at London University, six on "Dryden and his Times";
three on Swift; one on the period following Swift; and one each
on Wordsworth, Cowper, Scott, language, and the development of
English literature survive in more or less complete form. Clough
concentrates on Dryden and the writers who succeeded him,
commenting several times that it is unfortunate that his contemporaries know so little of the literature of that century. While very
careful not to overrate Dryden, he is anxious to establish his
importance as the great model for subsequent English prose, and
he is very much concerned that the essential sanity reflected in
the prose and poetry of Dryden and his eighteenth-century suc-
cessors be justly valued.

His sympathy with the eighteenth century is also reflected in the essay on Wordsworth. His admiration remains, but it is now tempered by an insistence that much of what Wordsworth wrote was poor; that "there is in Wordsworth's poems something of a spirit of withdrawal and seclusion from, and even evasion of the actual world"; and that the "exclusive student of Wordsworth goes away I fear with the strange persuasion that it is his business to walk about in this world of life and action and, avoiding life and action, have his gentle thoughts excited by flowers and running waters and shadows on mountain sides." Nor can Clough overlook that, as he points out with a twinkle, the poet was "apt to wind up his short pieces with reflection upon the way in which hereafter he expects to reflect upon his present reflections." [4] The movement of Clough's mind toward a solid and irreducibly severe set of responses to the world is nowhere better shown than in these remarks grounded perhaps in his discovery of the irrelevance of Wordsworth's faith to his own problems (as reflected for instance in "Blank Misgivings").

Clough's "Recent English Poetry," under which title he reviewed volumes of poetry by Matthew Arnold, Alexander Smith, and others, is chiefly of interest for the light it throws on the relationship with Arnold and is treated at length in the final chapter. There is, however, one most revealing paragraph toward the end of that rather diffuse review: his scornful summation of William Sidney Walker's *Poetical Remains.* Clough's unusual gentleness is attested by his friends' memoirs and his own letters; only in this one instance did he write anything for publication which betrayed personal antagonism:

> If our readers wish to view real timidity, real shrinking from actual things, real fear of living, let them open the little volume of Sidney Walker's Poetical Remains. The school-fellow and college friend of Praed, marked from his earliest youth by his poetic temper and faculty, he passed fifty-one years, mostly in isolation and poverty, shivering on the brink, trembling and hesitating upon the threshold of life. Fearful to affirm anything, lest it haply might be false; to do anything, because so probably it might be sin; to speak, lest he should lie; almost, we might say, to feel, lest it should be a deception,—so he sat, crouching and cowering, in the dismal London back-street lodging, over the embers of a wasting and dying fire, the true image of his own vitality. "I am vext," is his weak and complaining cry. . . .[5]

He obviously dislikes Walker's self-pity, but even more he dislikes what he regards as a shrinking from the real world—a fault from which he could not absolve even Wordsworth—and a trembling indecision. One can hardly avoid finding that the vehemence of this attack springs from Clough's aversion to qualities only lately exorcised from himself. It may have been unkind of Clough to condemn Walker for having lived his fifty-one years among fears which Clough knew only too well, but the real target of his disapproval is not Walker but the "fear of living." "Fearful to affirm anything, lest it haply might be false; to do anything, because so probably it might be sin" could well have been written of Clough by one of his detractors. The parallel is not altogether sound, for Clough had never sat "crouching and cowering," hugging his misery to himself (and the spectacle of Walker's doing so probably especially irritated him); he had faced his doubts and fears until he had conquered them. He was, however, so newly freed from a form of the malaise he sees in Walker that he could not behold it without reacting violently.

In his literary essays the subject to which Clough most often recurs is, as has been noted, the problem of translation. In addition to the "Illustrations of Latin Lyrical Metres," the essay "On Translating Homer," a considerable portion of the sixth lecture on Dryden, and almost all of his review of Aytoun and Martin's *Poems and Ballads of Goethe* treat this question and make the same general points. These points are that it is impossible to be both accurate and readable in a translation; that Dryden's translation of Virgil, like Pope's of Homer, could not fail to be misleading because the spirit of the later man was altogether different from that of the earlier; and—the central idea in "On Translating Homer"—that English hexameters cannot reproduce the effect of the Classical hexameter.

It is a minor puzzle why Clough continued to be interested in discussing a problem to which he believed there was no adequate solution, and, more importantly, continued to experiment with translating Homer into the English hexameters he judged so inadequate to the task. One may, however, use these preoccupations as one more bit of evidence for two assertions about Clough already made: first, that he wrote poetry only for diversion when not as a supplement to the development of his thought, and thus never aimed primarily at producing a pleasing object of art for others' delight; second, that his mind hesitated to dismiss an unresolved problem even when he felt that no resolution was possible.

III *Economics and Social Progress*

Clough's mature writing on economics consists of five letters published in *The Balance* (a London weekly) in 1846; the pamphlet on the Oxford Retrenchment Association; five incomplete drafts (including two "Letters of Parepidemus"); and a review of Charles Eliot Norton's *Considerations of Some Recent Social Theories* which appeared in the *North American Review*. Only two of these can properly be described as carefully prepared essays, but his thought, despite some evidence of a lessening adherence to Carlyle, is consistent within the whole group.

The reader who turns to Clough's treatments of economic problems to discover what practical remedies are proposed will be disappointed, nor will he find anything which may properly be regarded as a theory of economics or of society. At a first reading, these essays and letters seem, puzzlingly, to be constantly slipping away from the central issue, perversely refusing to come to the point and state what should be done about economic injustice or how private property should be regarded. The reason is that Clough is not an economist but a moralist; he is not outlining the proper economic structure but the attitude each individual should hold toward it. Of course, if each individual considered economic justice before buying or selling any item, however large or small, and if he regulated his business activities in accordance with fairness to the greatest number, the economic basis of society would be utterly changed. But to advocate such doctrines is not to propose an economic theory—economics is the science of structuring an economy so that certain results are brought about by laws, rules, and customs which the individual may violate only at his peril.

Clough's appeal to individual morality is clearly seen in his first two letters to *The Balance*. The first, fully agreeing that the repeal of the Corn Laws "will be economically a blessing" and perhaps productive of important social and moral benefits, urges that, nevertheless, since an economic change produces changes in the "moral life" of all those it affects, immediate steps should be taken to counteract any evil that can be anticipated from the change: ". . . social changes of some kind assuredly there will be; nor will they, of course, be unmixedly either good or evil. It is but prudence to think beforehand what they will be on either side, and seek to be prepared to avail ourselves of the good, and provide against the evil." [6]

Except for a brief reference to the possibility of some farm laborers having to turn to factories, Clough singles out no specific evil which he expects to follow from the repeal—and no special class to be protected from adverse effects. Rather, he simply seeks to warn readers of the *Balance* of their moral responsibilities in regard to the possible effects of the repeal. The appearance of such an admonitory letter amid the popular acclamation for the repeal reminds one of the counsels of Arnold against blind enthusiasm and partisanship in *Culture and Anarchy*.

The second letter was suggested by another contributor's letter urging that the principles of political economy are an important study for Christians who wish to apply Christian principles to society. Clough agrees, and develops the distinction between the use of political economy as a means of determining how to make money and its use as a means of determining a man's duties to society:

The first thought of an honest man on entering into a new position is to discover the obligations it entails on him. I receive a certain pay; do I do the work it is given for? I have fellow men to serve and assist me; do I pay them the wages of their work? Does the whole payment fall on me, and, if not, what is the proportion? Even so, it would seem, is it incumbent on each individual citizen to make out his position in the great economical system of the nation.[7]

The purpose of economics for Clough is to provide *moral* guidance—by understanding the economic system one may learn how to live morally within it. His position appears naïve, and it is from the point of view of a downtrodden economic group which desires political power in order to force through laws to protect itself. But Clough is not writing for the members of such a group—he is writing for the privileged classes and is assuming that their sense of *noblesse oblige,* if not their Christianity, encourages them to consider the good of the total society and that all they require is to see the situation accurately.

In the second letter he attacks as a common fallacy the principle that extravagance is good to the extent that it provides work

and an example of the rewards of industry. The idealistic economic reformer, of whatever class, will also find Clough's position
naïve. Why talk of deducing moral principles from accepted economic principles when the latter should themselves be based on
the former? What is needed is a reformation of the economic system based on moral values. Clough touches on this point in the
third of his letters on political economy: "It seems probable
enough that the commonly conceived rules of Political Economy
may be most materially modified by looking at its principles from
the higher point of justice and honesty," [8] but he refuses to go
beyond his original position. He is, in effect, leaving to those who
engage in politics the problem of adjusting the economic system
—an endless process in a field where no final and totally just system is likely to be devised—in order to consider simply what the
individual man of good will should do.

Clough's conscientiousness is nowhere better shown than in
these letters to *The Balance*. We may detect a singular innocence
in his belief that the privileged classes on the whole are sensitive
to the demands of justice and fairness, and we may very well feel
that for few besides Clough would it be possible continually to be
calculating the exact degree of equity in every transaction. A very
nice discrimination would have to be made to determine how
much continuing trade one should give to the present purveyors
of luxury in justice for their having been led to expect custom, and
how much should be withheld to avoid encouraging new workers
from entering the field; but Clough suggests that just such a determination ought to be made by each man. Nevertheless, in suggesting the necessity of such calculations, Clough was taking seriously the responsibilities of wealth and Christianity as generally
understood in his own time, and even in the twentieth century;
and if one finds the result ridiculous, the hollowness exposed is not
in Clough's view but in the pretensions of Western culture. *The
Balance* was after all intended to combat "a depraved and demor-
alizing Sunday-press" by making a specifically Christian appeal,
and Clough's interest in what was for him the unwonted activity
of writing to a newspaper is perhaps to be traced to his sense of
the need for looking at such areas as economics from a specifically
Christian view.

Underlying Clough's whole position is, finally, the insistence
that the entire economic system exists as a means of insuring men

a fair return for the work they do and that it is an imperfect expedient which requires constant correction in response to the claims of justice. Clough thus ends the last of the letters: "In the spirit of this finer justice and recognition of public duty, let us, as servants and hired workmen, ask ourselves each one of us,—What do I do for the pay I receive?" [9] In Clough's letters to Blanche from America, written in the midst of his anxiety over earning enough to marry and support a wife, he debates the worth to society of various kinds of jobs; one finds here evidence of the seriousness with which he regarded this question.

"A Consideration of Objections Against the Retrenchment Association," already discussed as exemplary of some of Clough's defects as an essayist, is essentially a reworking of *The Balance* letters. In the essay, he addresses to the undergraduates of Oxford his arguments against spending money for self-gratification and luxury, and attacks the position that the spending of money is in itself of benefit to the whole nation. The pamphlet echoes the letters in most particulars, assuming that "whoever is born into the world has a just claim to demand therein and therefrom work and wages for work"; but it goes beyond them in arguing that, as all man's needs are provided by the earth, the earth cannot be finally appropriated by individual owners: "for meat and drink and all things there is one sole machine, not made with hands, not capable of duplication, this terraqueous globe that moves incommunicably tied to one unchanging orbit." [10]

The same assertion is phrased in his "Letter on the Rights of Property" in another way: "The Land belongs to the human race that is, and that shall be; and whatever A, B and C have got out of it is liable to pay rent or royalties to the true proprietor." [11] And in one of the more happily phrased portions of the *Letter of Parepidemus*, "Might versus Right," Clough gives another formulation: "land, it is my belief, does by the appointment of Him who made it belong to that one of his servants who, for the common good, can turn it to the best account." [12] This statement is qualified by a warning to those who presume that they have a right to take what they want because they are more competent: "Though your bill be endorsed by the Honourable East India Company, the Czar Nicholas, the Emperor Napoleon, and heaven knows how many other high titled serene and most Christian Dei-gratiâ usurpers—

when finally it comes to be presented for payment you know to whom—Shall you feel quite safe of its being honoured?—" [13]

Unfortunately, in applying the argument of the letters to the specific question of the Oxford Retrenchment Association, Clough employed much more baroque phrasing than in his "Letters" and thus produced a pamphlet both tedious and overwrought. Indeed, there are passages that might lead one to suspect that Clough's satirical bent had for the moment gotten the best of him and had led him ino an unconscious choice of self-satirizing phrasing. Such is the following passage on whether the undergraduate should pay his debts to tradesmen (Bennett and Bickerstaff) before contributing to the relief of the Irish: "What then! truly, indeed, if Bennett and Bickerstaff are not famishing and may as well wait, why, you may as well not go to the opera, and pay your opera's price to keep your countrymen alive. But do not suppose it is I who so advise. Pay your debts by all means. Surprise Bennett with bank notes, and gratify Bickerstaff with gold." [14]

The suspicion that Clough sees all sides of a question so readily that at times he is led into phrasing an opposing position as strongly as his own and at other times into undercutting his arguments with invitations to their ironical reading is strengthened by several other pieces of Clough's prose. The third of the letters to *The Balance*, which leaves the question of political economy to consider Christian objections to serving in the militia, comes close to presenting the arguments against serving as strongly as those in favor. When into the mouth of the opponent is put "Endurance never runs the risk of defeat, and for her victories, how pure and how perfect," doubtless one is supposed to see the exaggeration of such an idealistic position; but in the statement of the other side— "Yet it may be, and I have heard it well stated, on the other hand, that strength and skill, and even standing armies, are gifts of God —talents entrusted to us"—the same ironic imp seems peeping over the phrase "even standing armies," inviting one to read this also as an exaggeration or parody.

The precise impulse behind Clough's "Address on Socialism," apparently addressed to the Council of the Society for Promoting Working Men's Associations, is puzzling. The basic argument is that, valuable as may be the cooperative establishments set up by the Council, it is a great error to believe that their Christian-

Socialist movement could eradicate the evils of society even were its doctrines imposed. The argument, phrased in a satiric tone more biting than any used against upper-class luxury, seems hardly what one would expect from Clough.

> For what is it you wish to clear away? The scandal of eating and drinking and unequal apportionments? Ah no, But the crying wrongs; the bitter tears of helpless oppression; the burning sense of injustice, and, its child, the cruel lust for retaliation! Will you annihilate also the grandeurs and elevations of righteous scorn, the glories and serenities of magnanimous forgiveness, the fervent reparation of repentance, and *its* child the generous warmth of mutual recognition? . . . —Ah but starvation; or if not starvation, what is worse, a life-long degradation; the demoralization of faith; the dram-drinking of hopelessness, the debauchery of recklessness.—And you will eradicate all these things, Halleluia, by cooperative workshops! Halleluia! For the Lord Omnipotent reigneth.—[15]

The explanation is that Clough's distrust of doctrines, economic as well as religious, is speaking here. Evil and unhappiness will not disappear no matter what social scheme is tried—the acceptance of life with all its imperfections in the "Mystery of the Fall" and in other poems written at approximately this time is the religious statement of this belief—but evil and injustice can be minimized in a society in which each man acts according to his own informed and carefully nurtured conscience. Nevertheless, one wonders whether Clough did not, as so often in his poems, simply abandon himself to the devil's advocate and try to balance his idealism by as strong a statement of the unidealistic view of economics as he could manage:

> O dear! It would be nicer certainly if nobody ever cheated us, or injured us, or insulted us, or despised us, or was unkind to us or rough to us or did anything we didn't like to us! But whether it would be better for us, in the end is really quite another question.—
> But suppose I win! Like a delicate player of cards shall I refuse the stakes?— To offer the sum back to your antagonist is an insult. And after all is it really worth so very much? These objects of competition—are they the great prizes? his or mine[—]what matters it? "Who steals my purse steals trash" Etc.—If a native superiority has given me my advantage, it is fitting I should accept it; if fortune as

I had [illegible word] always suspect, has had a great hand in it; still it is natural and right to a great extent to avail oneself of that too.[16]

"Like a delicate player of cards shall I refuse the stakes?" Clough had answered "yes" in one of the letters to *The Balance* in urging that unfair economic profit be regarded as an evil: ". . . with the knowledge that it is an evil—an unfairness—would arise, I think, both the wish and power to mitigate it. The advantage might at times be even waived; it would often surely be possible not to push it to the utmost; at the very least we should be spared the chuckling of the successful gamester, the boasting over good bargains; we should have in its stead the hope to find an occasion, some day and some way, of making amends." [17] The "no" which Clough gives in the "Address on Socialism" is, therefore, clearly an ironic corrective to the position he consistently maintains elsewhere. But of course, if the letter were ever actually sent, the recipients would have had no means of knowing this. One doubts that it was sent; certainly it was not intended for publication.

The position which both his poetry and prose indicate Clough had reached in the years around 1850 is summed up in his review of Charles Eliot Norton's *Considerations on Some Recent Social Theories*. The book was an analysis of the meaning of the theory that the people are the final interpreters of the will of God and of the cry for "Universal Liberty." Clough and Norton apparently shared many economic and religious views though their mutual influence cannot now be assessed. Clough fully approved Norton's argument that there is no perfect form of government and no meaning in the demand for complete liberty. Certainly Norton's premises and arguments are very close to the ones Clough had expressed before as well as after he met Norton. In the review, Clough's distrust of doctrine, disbelief in the possibility of an earthly Utopia, and dislike of man's selfish demands for happiness all combine in his ironic description of the hope which springs eternal:

The dream and aspiration of the ardent and generous spirits of our time is for a certain royal road to human happiness. Disappointed a thousand times, they still persist in their exalted creed that there must and will be here on earth, if not now, in some future and approaching time, a state of social arrangements in which the spontaneous action and free development of each individual constituent member will combine to form "a vast and solemn harmony," the ultimate perfect movement of collective humanity. There beautiful thoughts will distil as the dew, and fair actions spring up as the green herb; there, without constraint, we shall all be good, and without trouble, happy. . . . A divine interior instinct will intimate to each single human being his fittest and highest vocation, and will prompt and inspire and guide him to fulfill it; while in the pursuit of his own free choice, and in the fulfillment of his own strongest desires, he will, by the blessing of the presiding genius of humanity, best serve the true interests of Society and the Race.[18]

One hears in this passage Clough's own adieu to certain of his earlier expectations: he had himself hoped "a divine interior instinct" would one day lead him to "his fittest and highest vocation . . . and prompt and inspire and guide him to fulfill it." But, though no such interior instinct ever offers itself, there is a guide: "As a general rule of life and conduct, we see as yet no reason to believe that *liberty* . . . is better than service," and a few pages later "*Service*" is designated the "highest political watchword." As in the poems of these years, Clough has returned to the Doctrine of Work, but in a more chastened form than Carlyle's. God's toleration of the evil of the world is a mystery, as are his purposes for the world and even for each individual—to none are vouchsafed special instructions—but there is no doubt about the general order: all are here to work and serve.

In Clough's approving citation of the words of Marshal Bugeaud quoted by Norton it is perhaps no exaggeration to see his own acquiescence in the order of society that he had questioned in the *Bothie*: "Absolute equality does not belong to this world. It is God himself who has determined this, since he has created men so different in power, in intelligence, in activity, in inclinations. The Socialists, afflicted at seeing misery often at the side of ease, and even of riches, pursue the chimera of perfect quality. They believe to have found it in association; they are deceived; they will obtain only an equality of misery." [19] Clough is not abandoning all idealism here—one must still work to alleviate misery and promote good, but without being disappointed that the world cannot once and always be put to rights. Moral idealism and practical realism appear incommensurable as universal principles, but one nevertheless works by the best light one has.

IV   *Religious Beliefs*

Of the three significant discussions of religious questions in Clough's prose, the review of *The Soul* has already been treated in connection with the resolution of Clough's religious doubts in the poems of the early 1850's. It makes three central points: (1) one is to believe his own soul, (2) the conscience should not be over-developed to the point that one fears to take any action because it may be sinful, and (3) the answer to the question of what positive action one should take is to be found by looking at the state of the world around one. The service of one's fellows thus becomes the worship of God.

But what Clough leaves out of his review is as significant as what he includes. He passes silently over Newman's polemical passages, his attack on the Roman Catholic Church, and his three latter chapters "Spiritual Progress," "Hopes Concerning Future Life," and "Prospects of Christianity," touching upon these chapters only to say that "a single reviewer in a single review can scarcely presume to go duly into" the question of what other religious principles can be proved corollaries of "Believe thine own soul." [20] More significantly, he does not so much criticize or analyze the two chapters—"Sense of Sin" and "Sense of Personal Relationship to God"—on which his review is based as use them as starting points for statements he wishes to make.

In the "Sense of Sin" Newman was primarily concerned to comfort those who are tortured by remorse at not having lived up to their knowledge of good and evil. Clough's comments on this chapter treat unreasonable fears about committing future sins. In discussing the "Sense of Personal Relation to God," Clough, who in a letter of 1853 defined mysticism as "letting feeling run on," [21] vehemently attacked those devotional practices intended to induce a mystical sense of communion even though Newman had counseled no such practices. It would seem that, stimulated by his agreement with Newman's central arguments that religion should address itself to the soul and not the intellect (Clough was by 1850 in the process of abandoning the attempt to solve religious doubts by intellectual analysis) and that historical accounts of

Christ's life were not the essential grounds of faith, Clough had used the volume as a springboard for an expression of his own beliefs. The "Review" tells more about Clough's beliefs at this time than about Newman's book.

To the religious principles enunciated in the "Review" Clough adds several more. One of these, the subject of the brief "Paper on Religion," is that of "Silence." Mrs. Clough inserted this fragment in the midst of the review of *The Soul* when both were first published. Whether there was any authority for combining the two in some manner or other it is now impossible to know; but, despite a difference in tone, the two grow out of the same complex of religious beliefs. In the four paragraphs of this fragment Clough satirizes those who base their belief on versions of the cosmological argument, especially those versions which emphasize the order and regularity discovered by science, counselling "You have found out God[,] have you? Ah my friends! let us be—*Silent*." [22] With that precept Clough is opposing not simply the cosmological argument as refurbished by science, but all attempts to explain God or His relationship to the universe—a precept which, one notices, Clough obeyed in his review of *The Soul*, where it finds expression in his diffidence about considering further the principle which Newman claims to find in his own soul. "We presume neither to doubt nor to dogmatize.—" [23]

In the light of this principle, such a poem as Clough's "Hymn not a Hymn" (ὕμνος ἄυμνος) appears less tentative in its affirmation. In that poem, which he described in May, 1853, as "on the whole in sense very satisfactory to me still," [24] Clough is not being coy about his own faith in the existence of God, but sternly refusing to move beyond that of which his soul assures him into the realm of dogma and doctrine:

> O thou, in that mysterious shrine
> Enthroned, as we must say, divine!
> I will not frame one thought of what
> Thou mayest either be or not.
> I will not prate of 'thus' and 'so',
> And be profane with 'yes' and 'no.'
> Enough that in our soul and heart
> Thou, whatsoe'er thou may'st be, art.

The third of Clough's religious statements is the "Notes on the Religious Tradition" which takes the form of a series of assertions which are to serve as basic principles. The opening two paragraphs state in concise form the problems which had troubled so many serious undergraduates and young clergymen:

> It is impossible for any scholar to have read, and studied and reflected without forming a strong impression of the entire uncertainty of history in general—and of the history of the origin of Christianity in particular.
>
> It is equally impossible for any Man, to live, act, and reflect without feeling the significance and depth of the moral and religious teaching which passes amongst us by the name of Christianity.[25]

The "Notes" must be read by anyone who wishes to understand the position to which Clough had come; it sums up almost all points made elsewhere in the prose and poetry of these years. Thus it presents in two successive paragraphs Clough's denial of the importance of the historical evidence and his feeling that it is nevertheless folly to debate the point:

> . . . I see [not] how any one who will not tell lies to himself can dare to affirm that the narrative of the Four Gospels is an essential integral part of that Tradition.—
>
> I do not see that it is a great and noble thing, a needful or very worthy service, to go about proclaiming that Mark is inconsistent with Luke, that the first Gospel is not really Matthew's nor the last with any certainty John's—that St. Paul is not Jesus, etc., etc., etc.[26]

Refusing to make dogmatic statements to support the certainty of the beliefs he thinks yet remain, he admits, with a touch of irony, that "it may be that the facts which we, by the best force of our intellects discern are by his ordinance delusions intended of a set purpose to tempt us from our highest path—that of His Love and the Worship of him." But, on the other hand, as he argues in a manner reminiscent of Bishop Butler's *Analogy*, "Yet it is conceivable also that Sense and Mind, that Intellect and Religion, things without and things within are in harmony with each other." [27] On this possibility, which the speculative intellect can neither deny nor affirm, but for which a faith is grounded in the evidence of his own soul, Clough takes his stand, asking, as in the closing lines of the Seven Sonnets: "And with being here, doth palsy-giving fear,/ Whoe'er can ask, or hope accord the best."

On this ground Clough affirms his acceptance of what he calls the "great Religious Tradition." Of what that tradition consists is never made entirely explicit, nor can it be; as the whole essay implies, it will not be entirely the same for any two men. It is to be found "neither in Rationalism nor in Rome"; it is to be searched for in experience, in reason, and in our knowledge of past thought and lives. It is found above all, says Clough, in experience, especially that which comes from work and service. It is to be found in reason, for, though reason cannot guarantee beliefs (the attempt to do so is Rationalism), one is not called upon to believe anything contrary to reason. This statement explains Clough's "I believe that I may without any such perversion of my reason, without any such mortal sin against my own soul, which is identical with reason; and against the Supreme Giver of that soul and reason, still abide by the real Religious Tradition." [28]

The Religious Tradition may also be found in voices from the past:

The Religious Tradition—as found everywhere, as found not only among clergymen and religious people, but among all who have really tried to order their lives by the highest action of the reasonable and spiritual will. I will go to Johnson, I will go to Hume, as well as to Bishop Butler. . . . Every rule of conduct, every maxim, every usage of life and society must be admitted, like Ecclesiastes of old in the Old Testament, so in each new Age to each new Age's Bible.[29]

This passage echoes Clough's earlier reference to the wisdom of Hume, Butler, and Johnson in "resting upon only the lowest grounds." It also calls to mind another parallel: Clough is essentially appealing to that "best that has been thought and said" upon which Matthew Arnold rested his hope for the improvement of mankind.

Clough's final point in this, his last known writing on religious topics, exhibits the continuing influence of Dr. Arnold. Arnold strove above all for a broad church embracing all Christians; Clough, who extends this position, argues that each man must be granted the "form of truth" that will suit his "peculiar nature" as formed by "climate, parentage, and other circumstances . . . too strong for us":

It is very true that, speaking generally, to a certain extent we must all of us be of the religion of our fathers; we are so, whether we like it or not;—whether we say we are, or say we are not. It is very true nevertheless that we cannot refuse to know when we are told it on good authority that there are many more Buddhists in the world than there are Christians.—And it appears to me that it is much more the apparent dispensation of things that we should gradually widen than that we should narrow and individualize our creeds.[30]

Despite their faults, Clough's essays have a salutary soundness about them. If his economic views are in one sense impractical in their idealism, they avoid, on the other hand, the impracticability which comes from the attempt to apply sweeping generalizations to specific situations; he constantly tries to analyze the given situation and to adjust his beliefs to it. Similarly, if his religious tenets seem too vague to serve as a bulwark against the evils of this world, they avoid that dissipation of force in controversy which is inevitable in a more complex body of doctrine. His final position in both fields illustrates the fear that, the more sweeping a generalization, the less truth there is in it and the more force there is in the arguments against it. His previously unpublished rough draft of the conversation between the young dog and his uncle puts this as succinctly as possible:

The young cur one day observed to the elderly sheep dog his Uncle. It is clear to me that in themselves, and in the idea all dogs are equal. Nay, thank God replied the other that there are some neither as ugly as me nor as silly as you.—Some time afterwards the young cur in a more thoughtful temper resumed. Circumstances it is obvious exercise a most powerful influence. Early habits and associations; locality; education; good or bad company; what one sees and what one has to do. It cannot of course be expected that I who live with the lower orders and go running after sheep should be what I should, of myself be, under more favouring circumstances. From circumstances ensue great distinctions: but originally and in themselves I have no doubt that all dogs are equal.

In the same way it would seem to me an obvious conclusion, replied the other, that originally and in themselves all circumstances are equal. It is a good thing to be cleanly, and yet at the same time how pleasant dirt is. The young cur did not see the cogency of this.—[31]

CHAPTER 8

Return to Poetry: Mari Magno

THE tales which comprise *Mari Magno* were written during the last year of Clough's life while he was travelling abroad hoping to recruit his strength. None of them received a final revision, and at least one was left quite incomplete; it is difficult to know, therefore, what changes Clough might have made had he lived. Nevertheless, since each tale is completed to the extent of having a beginning, middle, and end, there is no question as to the kind of stories Clough wished to tell at the time they were written; short of radical rewriting, Clough's changes could have been only for the purpose of polishing.

Much of the poem is taken from experience. The voyage itself was suggested by his 1852 trip to America; the narrators of the tales were probably partially modeled on Clough's fellow-passengers, the author drawn from Lowell, the lawyer from Thackeray.[1] In "The Lawyer's First Tale" the visit to the cousins was, we are told in the "Memoir," a reflection of Clough's visits to his uncles' homes during Rugby holidays.[2] Emily's advice to her cousin not to remain at college and to think of marriage, cited approvingly by the narrator of "The Lawyer's First Tale," seems to represent Clough's retrospective verdict on his decision to leave Oxford: it was right. The doubts about marriage so fully developed by the youth of "The Clergyman's Tale" can hardly be read in any other way than as a reflection of Clough's own doubts about committing himself in marriage. His letters to Blanche certainly betray considerable anguishing self-analysis (commented on rather fully by Lady Chorley), and there are the hints (see Chapter 3) that perhaps Blanche was not the first woman to cause Clough to turn his mind toward the analysis of a possible marriage. A number of the scenic details, especially in "My Tale," seem to have been derived from his travels during the time he was writing *Mari Magno*.

The history of critical commentary on these poems is easily summarized. They received generally very high praise when first published in the 1862 and 1863 editions of the *Poems* (the 1863 edition included more, though not all, of the tales), eliciting favorable comparisons with Chaucer and Crabbe. But the poem has dated more than anything else of Clough's, including the *Bothie*, and his twentieth-century admirers tend to ignore it as much as possible.

The external structure is derived from the *Canterbury Tales*, and the directness of style owes much to Crabbe (we know from Clough's letters that he had been reading and delighting in Crabbe in 1865),[3] but the substance of the tales and the whole manner of their telling lack Crabbe's realism and Chaucer's wide sympathy and humor. Clough's choice of genre seems most unfortunate. There had been few enough successful short narratives in either prose or verse in English literature since Chaucer—even in prose the brief tale or short story would not begin to flourish in England until the 1880's and 1890's when the peculiar requirements of the brief narrative would be recognized. Moreover, Clough's handling of narrative had never been notable even where he had allowed himself larger scope—he was wise in focusing *Dipsychus* almost entirely on the tension between intellectual positions rather than on action. It was another mistake for a man whose idealism had always been at war with his sense of the real to attempt to follow Crabbe, as well as for a man who had objected to Chaucer's coarseness to use the *Canterbury Tales* as a model.[4]

I *The Themes*

What does *Mari Magno* indicate about Clough's outlook some seven years after settling into his position as examiner, marrying, and almost completely abandoning the writing of original poetry? The conventional morality and generally sentimental tone of the tales have led many of Clough's critics to argue that the influence of his wife, with her rigidly orthodox mind and circumscribed sympathies, had deadened Clough's sensibilities and undermined his ability to see through the superficial and meretricious.

Indeed, Blanche Clough's own remarks have generally been read as revealing that some such process had been at work. Writing to the Reverend Percival Graves in 1865 about "Dipsychus Con-

tinued," which in its conventional outlook toward sexual sins is
much like *Mari Magno,* Mrs. Clough commented that Clough
"did change enough to make me think he would have gone further." Evidently regarding the continuation as having been written much longer after *Dipsychus* than Lady Chorley's discoveries
would indicate, Mrs. Clough then remarks that the continuation,
"tho' most unsatisfactory, was a sort of returning to commonplace
views as having a degree of truth in them." [5]

But if one is to imagine Clough, at the time of writing *Mari
Magno,* to have been thinking back on his life and seeing some
sort of pattern in it, that pattern takes a somewhat different form
than Mrs. Clough appears to have understood. Though the sense
of morbid guilt which Clough gives to the erring husband of "The
Clergyman's Second Tale" reflects a fierce commitment to rigor-
ously pure moral standards, one must remember that in the matter of sexual relationships Clough's position had always been se-
verely chaste. In the midst of questioning God's purposes and
even existence, he had never questioned the rightness of the moral
code, particularly on this point. Indeed, if Clough perchance felt
that he had at some time erred, however venial his sin might seem
to other eyes, the guilt he would have felt would easily explain
"Dipsychus Continued" and "The Clergyman's Second Tale." As
for the rest of the tales of *Mari Magno,* there is a different explanation: they seem indeed to represent a resolution of some of
Clough's earlier uncertainties, but not in quite the fashion Mrs.
Clough had in mind.

Not only do all the tales of *Mari Magno,* with one exception,
deal with marriage, as one might expect from the title, but the
entire poem also implies a certain attitude toward it. First, in
every case, the man's decision to marry the girl results in happiness, but, in the two cases in which the man irresolutely hesitates
until too late, he realizes that he has made an error. "The American's Tale," with the subtitle "Juxtaposition," not only recalls the
fears of Claude in *Amours* that what seemed love was merely
juxtaposition, but presents a case in which a chance juxtaposition
leads to a happy marriage. Moreover, "The American's Tale" is
preceded by a tale in which the lover's doubts are resolved by
a chance meeting which precipitates an impulsive marriage, and
is followed by the "Mate's Tale" which describes a most hasty
and unlikely marriage between a ship's captain and a French girl

who finds herself stranded without resource in an English port. Both marriages prove successful.

The key to all of these stories of marriage is to be found in the contrast between the first two tales. The "Lawyer's First Tale" describes the folly of the young man who was too slow to recognize his love for a cousin. The "Clergyman's First Tale," subtitled "Love is fellow service," describes a man and a woman perplexed by doubts as to whether they are truly in love—after having dallied away their opportunity and found themselves parted, they meet by chance and marry before they have time for much reflection. Their doubts evaporate in the light of experience, and the brief account of their marriage seems to argue that happiness is not something which is to be deserved by patiently waiting, however purely and seriously, for the mate approved by a sign from the sky, but by working practically toward it, and thus meriting perhaps even more than had been hoped for:

> Yet in the eye of life's all-seeing sun
> We shall behold a something we have done,
> Shall of the work together we have wrought,
> Beyond our aspiration and our thought,
> Some not unworthy issue yet receive;
> For love is a fellow-service I believe.
>
> (341)

That the man of the "Lawyer's Second Tale," having by procrastination lost his first love, is able to make later an apparently happy marriage seems to support the above conclusion by denying the romantic belief implicit in *Ambarvalia*, especially in "When patient sighs the bosom fill," that there is for each man only one love which is "the veritable thing."

Second, there is in *Mari Magno* not only a most idealistic set of portraits of women—one only whose unthinking delight in dalliance makes her vicious—but a reiterated affirmation of the intuitive wisdom of women and of their power of healing the infirmities of the male mind and soul. The belief in the wisdom of women had indeed been a favorite one of Clough's at least since the *Bothie;* Philip finds Elspie to possess a greater wisdom than he has been able to draw from much reading, and Claude is astonished at Mary's understanding which never gives way "to

those vain/Conscious understandings that vex the minds of mankind." [6] But this belief is stated even more positively in the
"Lawyer's First Tale":

> For all I read and thought I knew,
> She simply looked me through and through.
> Where had she been, and what had done,
> I asked, such victory to have won?
> She had not studied, had not read,
> Seemed to have little in her head,
> Yet of herself the right and true,
> As of her own experience, knew.
>
>   (317)

There is the one exception whose place in the rank of women is
established by Clough's conventionally deprecating description:
". . . a poor flaunting creature of the town/In crumpled bonnet
and in faded gown/With tarnished flowers and ribbons hanging
down" (363). The remainder are wise, understanding and devoted to administering balm to the male (when the wife and
naïve former mistress of the man in the "Lawyer's Second Tale"
meet, after having "kissed and cried," both devote themselves to
comforting him).

In the light of these attitudes toward the power and grace of
women and the power of marriage to create happiness, one can
hardly avoid finding considerable meaning in the fact that "My
Tale" is the only one from *Mari Magno* that does not tell a story of
marriage. In it the narrator sketches a number of simple incidents
from his travels. Its closest connection with the tales of marriage is
the sketch of a peasant girl, briefly glimpsed and soon lost—a
closer connection than it first appears if Clough is here indulging
in a last allusion to a love far in the past which he had too much
analyzed and doubted until his chance was lost. The handling of
the theme of marriage in *Mari Magno* can thus be taken as adding
one more support to the arguments for believing that Clough was
involved in a mysterious romance in the Highlands, or in Italy, or
both.

II *The Absence of Tension*

The themes which run through *Mari Magno* do not coalesce
into a fully articulated position. But it does not seem an untenable

suggestion that there is a curious doubleness in the poem, the existence of which, hardly surprising in Clough's poetry, fails to
stand out clearly because the conflict has been resolved. It is at
least possible that Clough was both paying homage to a romance
of long ago (now seen perhaps as broken off unwisely) and at the
same time expressing the peace and happiness he has found in his
marriage. Surely, despite the evidence of *Mari Magno,* Clough
had not come to believe that all marriages, even those brought
about by pure "juxtaposition," should turn out well; rather, he was
forcefully repudiating his earlier overly analytical speculation
about how to recognize one's "destined" mate. Mrs. Clough might
have been somewhat wounded had she recognized the possibility
that part of *Mari Magno* was Clough's revaluation of an old love
affair, but she could well enough have been pleased with the
poem's affirmation of the doubt-resolving success of his marriage
to her. The happiness he had found in his marriage had dissolved
his earlier skepticism about love and had replaced it with a romantic faith.

Mrs. Clough felt that but for Clough's early death *Mari Magno*
would have marked the beginning of a new poetic vein: "He had
to enter on a new line, to create a new treatment of old subjects,
to turn them over and bring them out in the new light of his
critical but kindly philosophy. This, in *Mari Magno,* he had begun
to do, and the rapid production of these last poems makes us believe that this new vein would have continued had he lived, and
that we should have received a further expression of his views
about the daily problems of social life." She later speaks of Clough
turning his mind "to the practical questions of the world." [7]

Others have also regretted that Clough was not granted a few
more years to develop his new poetic stance. But, though one cannot affirm positively that, had he lived, Clough would not have
produced better poetry than any he had written, there is little
basis for such a belief in the tales of *Mari Magno.* His whole later
view of life lies behind them, but it shines through so feebly that
it is not surprising to find both his defenders and detractors considering them no more than pleasant little tales.

Clough had taken his position in regard to poetry long before
Matthew Arnold charged him with having no "assiette." The
foundation of his poetry was conflict, and its interest lay in the
vividness with which he conveys that tension. Careful polishing

and refining were not necessary to this intention and might indeed have undercut it. The honesty of his poetry was guaranteed by its foundation in the conflicts of Clough's own mind. When the conflicts were resolved and he turned to new subjects, a new technique of poetic architecture was necessary. He might have achieved it, but the *Mari Magno* tales with their conventional themes and rough workmanship give no indication that he had yet begun to find his way. Nor was Clough in these poems actually turning toward "practical questions." His only "practical" advice in *Mari Magno* is not to try to anatomize love.

CHAPTER 9

Clough, Arnold, and a Perspective

A NY consideration of Clough's place in the stream of nineteenth-century thought leads almost inevitably to a discussion of his relationship to Matthew Arnold. Not only were they friends, and very close ones for a time, but a number of circumstances in their lives were similar. Dr. Arnold's influence on Clough was so strong, at least for a number of years, that Clough was almost as much his son as Matthew; and the Rugby headmaster's family did indeed provide a sort of home for Clough. Both took a Second Class degree but went on to become fellows of Oriel. Both startled readers by the unexpected tones of their first volumes of poetry. Both wrote poetry of a dark, questioning cast and were more concerned for substance than for the achievement of Tennysonian melody. Both avoided entering the Church but devoted large portions of their writing to wrestling with the problem of contemporary religious belief. There are reasons for suspecting that both had emotionally and poetically significant unsuccessful love affairs about which nothing can now be ascertained. And then, to make their relationship in the minds of later generations indissoluable, Clough was commemorated in one of Arnold's greatest poems.

I *The Contrast*

But "Thyrsis" did far more than forge a final link between the names of the two poets; it also established the perspective from which their relationship would largely be seen. Arnold would be perceived as the successful poet and thinker paying a melancholy tribute to his much less successful friend whose early death itself could be regarded, as it is in "Thyrsis," as symbolic of a failure of fortitude and will. Arnold is he who untiringly seeks the "fugitive and gracious light"; Clough is the "too quick despairer" who "of his own will went away."

The classic analysis of the differences between the two men is

that presented in Lionel Trilling's *Matthew Arnold*. Trilling interprets Arnold's insouciance and banter as providing a protective
hedge to keep his friends at a distance: "What Arnold feared in all
his friends, and especially in Clough, as the most intimate, was a
thing that he feared in himself. He perceived in his friends the
driving restless movement of the critical intellect trying to solve
the problem of the 19th century." [1] Arnold was thus trying to protect his own poetic power from the destructive demands of the
intellect. This interpretation would seem to explain the peculiari-
ties of Clough's poetry as well as those of Arnold's personality.
Arnold, aided perhaps by the almost inevitable reaction of a son
against a highly revered father, put aside critical analysis to concentrate on poetry; Clough, aided by the strong sense of duty in-
culcated by his mother, regarded any refusal to analyze basic
principles and to face the truth as a kind of sin; and thus intellectual speculation became the substance of his poetry.

But there is an additional point which must be made about this
comparison: Arnold was unable to sustain his poetic vision precisely because he had denied a necessary ingredient. In his well-
known essay, "The Function of Criticism at the Present Time," his
central argument is that the creative writer cannot create both
fresh ideas and their literary expression. To the extent that this is
true, and it seems to be at least partly so, Arnold was wise in
choosing to avoid philosophical speculation in favor of poetic expression. But, as Arnold wrote, those poets are especially fortunate who live in a time when a current of fresh ideas is flowing.
He himself, living when the philosophical waters were much
troubled and muddied, was as a poet doomed to express a fairly
personal sense of the despair in life which he could not transcend.
Thus it was that Arnold felt the poetic spring dry up so soon, and
was forced to move into the turmoil of contemporary thought:

> Ah me! this many a year
> My pipe is lost, my shepherd's holiday!
> Needs must I lose them, needs with heavy heart
> Into the world and wave of men depart;
> But Thyrsis of his own will went away.

Arnold's was the wiser decision for the man who wished to devote
himself to perfecting a poetic vehicle for the expression of an im-

mediate individual response to life; but, once this vein was mined, no other was discovered. One reads Arnold's poetry for the art and beauty with which it expresses Romantic melancholy stiffened by a kind of Classical Stoicism, and for the clarity with which he expresses what seems a prevailing mood in the later nineteenth century.

One reads Clough for a quite different reason: the expression of the struggle to retain old or find new bases of faith and belief. In choosing to use poetry as a means of working out, or at least clearly stating, his own perplexities, Clough made an unusual choice; but one most fortunate for the reader today. Had he been able to avoid critical analysis and devote himself to more lyrical poetry—something which there is little evidence he ever desired —readers would have been denied what is probably the most powerful record of the nineteenth-century clash between faith and skepticism. Had he chosen prose as his medium, the emotional overtones, the sense of the interplay between feeling and emotion which poetry captures, would have been lost. No man not actually in the throes himself could have portrayed the struggle with such faithfulness and intensity.

The work of a skillful poet regarding the struggle from without would have been no doubt much more finished, more technically polished, more accurate perhaps in phrasing, but some of the sense of struggle would have been lost. Arnold once wrote to his sister: "I feel bent against the modern English habit (too much encouraged by Wordsworth) of using poetry as a channel for thinking aloud, instead of making anything." [2] But, though he may have encouraged the kind of poetry Clough wrote, Wordsworth himself was, one must remember, recalling in tranquillity earlier emotions. When his poetry deals with a clash of viewpoints or concepts, it almost always summarizes that clash as having occurred and been resolved in the past. "Elegiac Stanzas," for instance, conveys a sense of resignation to the new viewpoint; the period of actual struggle is over. Wordsworth's poem is a more finished poem perhaps, than Clough ever wrote. But Wordsworth cannot, does not, give one the special quality for which one values Clough.

Arnold's phrase "instead of making anything" is significant. A distinction is often made between the poet as "maker" and the poet as "prophet." Clough was not a "maker" like Arnold; neither was he a "prophet" like Wordsworth. Instead, he painted the mental chaos which all thinking humans must now and then have felt around them. The world does not need an abundance of poets doing this—that would be intolerable—but to portray accurately the particular historical form that man's eternal uncertainty takes in one's own time is indeed valuable. Finally, it is only just to Clough to remember that—while he gives expression to the emotional and nonrational impulses which are concomitants and to some extent participants in internal debates—the debate and doubt, unlike so many of the personal emotional orgies of contemporary American poets, are given rational formulation. One knows, that is, what the turmoil is about.

Testimony to the strong personal bonds between Clough and Matthew Arnold and to the great differences in their approach to literature, morality, and speculative thought is to be found in Arnold's letters to Clough and in both men's letters to their families and friends (unfortunately, only one extant letter from Clough to Arnold is known to survive). Although they were particularly close during the years both were at Oxford, no letters between them are known from this period, probably because there would have been little occasion to write while seeing each other so constantly. But Arnold in his later letters refers to how much Clough had influenced him.[3] The picture which emerges from all accounts is of a very close personal relationship in which Arnold felt an intellectual indebtedness to Clough—as one would expect since Clough was four years the elder, a graduate and tutor who tried hard to prepare a somewhat dilatory Arnold for his examinations.

The earlier extant letters from Arnold to Clough exhibit an exuberant, highly mannered style that parodies Carlyle and becomes at times incomprehensible amid figures and allusions. Very likely Clough at this time affected the same style (his letters to Thomas Arnold maintain a similar tone, and his one surviving letter to Matthew is breezy enough) and wrote in the full confidence that his letters would be read by a kindred spirit. By 1847, however, Matthew Arnold's letters discussing Clough's poems (later to be printed in *Ambarvalia*) betray a harsher note, his criticism not directed so much against Clough's technical handling as against his attempt "to *solve* the Universe." [4] By 1848 the tension between them was acknowledged by both; Arnold begins a letter, "My heart warms to the kindness of your letter; it is necessity not inclination that ever repels me from you."[5]

Later in the year Arnold begins advising Clough on the necessity of making decisions about his life: "If you mean to do nothing why not emigrate? Shake yourself—it is easier to discover what we *can* do than our vanity lets us think. For God's sake don't mope, for from that no good can come."[6] In the next letter he questions whether there is such a thing as "the *right* way" for an individual, apparently replying to some expression of Clough's feeling that a man must wait for the right way to become clear. During this period Arnold's distaste for the critical questioning and all-doubting spirit he finds in Clough and others grew so strong that, as he admitted in a letter of 1853 to Clough, he had thought of estranging himself from such friends—"Barring out all influences that I felt troubled without advancing me."[7]

It was not only Clough's mood that troubled Arnold, but a strong distaste for his style. The *Bothie,* Clough's most sunny major poem, caused Arnold to think "I can, if need be, at last dispense with them all, even with him: better that, than be sucked for an hour even into the Time Stream in which they and he plunge and bellow."[8] Arnold followed up the writing of such a general judgment by putting his finger specifically on the failure of Clough's poems to achieve beauty through *form.* This is the result, he thinks, of "trying to go into and to the bottom of an object instead of grouping *objects.*"[9] The differences between Arnold and Clough are demonstrated by their attitudes on style. On its importance, they were both agreed; for both, style was far more than decoration.

If Arnold could consider breaking friendships over matters of style, Clough felt hardly less strongly. "Things really ill-written it does one a little harm to read," he wrote to Blanche *a propos* an article by James Martineau published in the *Westminster Review.*[10] But for Clough the great service of good style, as indicated in his London University lectures, is the accuracy with which it expresses things and, more, the writer's relation to them: "Style is the way of presenting things, and that will of course indicate the way in which people looked at things. By the description he gives you, you know where the describer stands. . . . Raphael's man-

ner of painting the Virgin and Child is more significant than the
fact that the Virgin and Child are what he paints." [11] An even
more important service of style is in making it possible to say certain things otherwise beyond the ordinary capacity of language:
"It may really be affirmed that some of the highest truths are only
expressible to us by style,—only appreciable as indicated by manner." [12] Arnold would scarcely have quarreled with either of the
above formulations, nor would Clough have quarreled with Arnold's goal of achieving beauty through style. But their emphases
are different, and Clough was content to forge his style as a tool
for giving accuracy to thought and giving shape to otherwise
amorphous complexities.

Despite such vigorously expressed differences, when the two
men were together in London, they generally breakfasted together twice a week until Arnold's marriage in 1851. We do not
know Clough's feelings about the relationship with Arnold; the
tone of Arnold's letters indicates that Clough was able to accept
Arnold's outbursts with some serenity. On the other hand,
Clough's letters in 1852 to Blanche and Arnold's answers to
Clough reflect a sense of injury at the way Arnold seemed to be
growing away from him. Arnold answered with a candid protesta-
tion: "remember that I am and always shall be, whatever I do or
say, powerfully attracted towards you, and vitally connected with
you." [13] From this point on, though Arnold is still at times critical
of Clough's work and refers again in November, 1853, to Clough's
fluctuations as his reason for having "to hold fast my rudder," [14]
there is a tone of strong affection in Arnold's letters—an affection
evident especially in his letters to his mother and to Blanche
Clough on Clough's death.

However, the evidence left us indicates that after 1852 Clough
rejected, if not Arnold the man, at least Arnold the poet of melancholy. Clough's "Recent English Poetry"—a review of Arnold's
Strayed Reveller and *Empedocles on Etna,* Alexander Smith's
Poems, and a volume of poems each by William S. Walker and
William Allingham published in the *North American Review* in
1853—is the best evidence of this rejection.[15] The review, devoted
primarily to Arnold and Smith, makes a number of its major
points by comparing the two poets. Giving no hint that he knows
to whom the initial under which Arnold hid his authorship refers,

Clough expresses no doubt that "A" has "a calmer judgment . . . a more poised and steady intellect . . . a finer and rarer aim perhaps, and certainly a keener sense of difficulty, in life." [16]

However, in comparing Smith's active optimism with Arnold's subtlety and melancholy, Clough, after two paragraphs of typically indecisive prose, plumps for "the picture of simple, strong, and certain . . . feelings" [17]—and he does so on the curiously Arnoldian grounds that such sentiments are at the time much more needed. Clough was not a great admirer of Smith, as a letter to Blanche written not long after reveals;[18] he was using Smith to clarify his reasons for disengaging his sympathies from the subtle, melancholy view he associates with Arnold. The review thus marks Clough's final preference for action over speculation.

As early as 1851 Clough had written to Blanche: "*The Strayed Reveller* you won't like. It had a great effect on me though, it and its writer, but it is over I hope and I don't mean to let it have any more. Do you know what is meant by 'mollis et exspes' (in Horace)? That is my feeling about it more recently." [19] Since Arnold in 1852 wrote Clough, *a propos Sohrab and Rustum,* "*You* in your heart are saying *mollis et exspes* over again," [20] it is likely that Clough had expressed a similar judgment about *The Strayed Reveller* directly to Arnold. That Arnold is in the same letter concerned to defend his analysis of the "*true blankness* and *barrenness,* and *unpoetrylessness*" of the time indicates that Clough's position had swung around to a condemnation of the cheerless or despairing in poetry—the position Arnold was to express in his Preface of 1853. By this time, it seems, Clough had worked through his speculative doubts and peremptorily dismissed them —at least insofar as they inhibited participation in the life around him.

II *Poetic Replies*

Bearing this history of the conflicts between Arnold and Clough in mind, it is not surprising to find challenges and replies to each other embodied in their poems. There are, of course, Arnold's three sonnets, first published in 1849, addressed to Clough as "A Republican Friend." The first expresses sympathy with Clough's republican sentiments; the second qualifies this sympathy with doubts about the efficacy of revolution within the limits afforded

by the "Mountains of Necessity"; and the third, "Religious Isolation," scolds Clough for wishing to find "the holy secret" of his life
in the external, natural world. These are not among Arnold's
really successful poems, however, nor do they much clarify the
larger differences between the poets.

More interesting is the implicit dialogue carried on by means of
parallel images which has been pointed out in recent years. The
total pattern of this imagery was at first seen by none of the scholars who commented on specific portions of it, and there are still
grounds for argument about the sequence in which the poems
concerned were written (and thus about who was answering
whom); but the number of parallels which have been noticed is
now so great that one can hardly doubt that the two men were
often replying to each other in their poetry.[21] Interestingly
enough, most of these passages make use of images drawn from
aspects of nature, especially the sea, around which both poets created their most lyrical poetry.

The most striking example is the sequence of similar images
which can be traced in Clough's *Bothie*, Arnold's "Dover Beach,"
and Clough's "Say not the struggle." In Section IX of the *Bothie*,
the following two passages, occurring within forty lines of each
other, call to mind the key images of "Dover Beach." The first
presents the heart of Hewson's doubt:

> If there is battle, 'tis battle by night: I stand in the dark-
> ness,
> Here in the mêlée of men, Ionian and Dorian on both sides,
> Signal and password known; which is friend and which is
> foeman?
>
> (170)

The second part of the "fragments again without date addressed
to Adam":

> As at return of tide the total weight of ocean
> Drawn by moon and sun from Labrador and Greenland,
> Sets-in amain, in the open space betwixt Mull and Scarba,
> Heaving, swelling, spreading, the might of the mighty At-
> lantic;
> . . . .

> So in my soul of souls through its cells and secret recesses,
> Comes back, swelling and spreading, the old democratic fer-
> > vour.
>
>   (171)

And from Arnold's "Dover Beach":

> And we are here as on a darkling plain
> Swept with confused alarm of struggle and flight,
> Where ignorant armies clash by night.

And:

> The Sea of Faith
> Was once, too, at the full, and round earth's shore
> Lay like the folds of a bright girdle furl'd;
> But now I only hear
> Its melancholy, long, withdrawing roar,
> Retreating, to the breath
> Of the night-wind, down the vast edges drear
> And naked shingles of the world.

The similar descriptions of the world as a dark, disordered battle-field on which friend cannot be distinguished from foe, and the opposed uses of the sea—one poet using the flowing tide as an image for a faith which at least at times comes to him, the other the ebb as the image for the loss of faith by a whole society—would by themselves strongly suggest that they are to be read as statement and reply between two close friends. Such a judgment becomes almost certain when it is pointed out that Clough's "Say not the struggle" also employs the image of a battle to protest that one should never say that the struggle is unavailing—the confusion of the battle may conceal an imminent victory. Moreover, in the same poem Clough returns to his image of the returning tide:

> For while the tired waves, vainly breaking,
> Seem here no painful inch to gain,
> Far back, through creeks and inlets making
> Come, silent, flooding in, the main.

Since (in the notebook in which he wrote out a number of his poems for Blanche) Clough appears to have assigned "Say not" to his stay in Rome in 1849, that date would seem all but established. The date of composition of "Dover Beach" has been a matter of debate (it was not published until 1867), but most scholars place it at least as late as 1851. Therefore, the otherwise attractive possibility that the *Bothie* was the earliest, "Dover Beach" a reply to it, and "Say not" written after Clough had seen a copy of Arnold's poem, must, though it has been urged, probably be dismissed. The fact of a kind of dialogue through images remains, however.

In addition, W. Stacy Johnson has pointed out that Clough and Arnold frequently employ images associated with water and that they very often employ these to speak to similar problems. Johnson points to the image of "islands joined beneath the sea" in Clough's "Truth is a golden thread" and in two of Arnold's poems, "Written in Butler's Sermons" and "To Marguerite—Continued." The imagery of the sundering sea and uniting arch link the same two Arnold poems with Clough's "The mighty ocean rolls and raves," and parallel uses (though often with conflicting statement) of the images of a river flowing to the sea or of ships navigating the ocean. To the instances cited by Johnson should be added the closing lines of Clough's "Away, haunt not thou me" in which the poet looks to "the strong current flowing,/Right onward to the Eternal Shore" and the lines in the third scene of "The Mystery of the Fall" in which Adam prophesies that, after "the straits of anguish and of doubt," Cain will reach "the calm ocean" which is the "consummated consciousness of self."

What is most remarkable about these parallels is that, in the majority of cases, it is Clough's version of a particular image that expresses the more optimistic view. Johnson, noting this tendency, finds that, nevertheless, "Clough is finally less certain of himself and of the world." Johnson contrasts Clough's

> Sails rent,
> And rudder broken,—reason impotent,—
> Affection all unfixed; so forth I fare
> On the mid seas unheedingly . . .

with Arnold's

> Ah: let us make no claims
> On life's incognizable sea,
> To too exact a steering of our way.

But it is important to notice that the Clough passage is taken from the "Blank Misgivings" sequence written about 1841.[22] Though both poets used the common images here cited to convey both hope and disillusion, Clough's contributions to this poetic dialogue, which one can date with either certainty or high probability to the years 1849–52, tend to take the more optimistic side—like the passages from the earlier *Bothie*. Clough's thought was moving away from sympathy with Arnoldian melancholy toward his own acceptance of a world which, despite the mysteries of God's purpose, "means good." Thus the image of "the calm ocean" as the assured goal of Cain and his descendants expresses perfectly the hopeful position Clough had finally achieved.

The attempts to read the poems of 1849–52 as reflecting the doubts and anguish of *Amours* and *Dipsychus* instead of as representing a return, in a deeper form, to the optimism of the *Bothie,* have been one reason that Clough has continued to be seen as a much gloomier poet than Arnold. Another is that, having virtually abandoned all writing in the years following his attainment of an intellectual peace, Clough provides nothing to compare with the urbane, positive later Arnold—the prose Arnold. Much as one may regret that Clough did not, could not perhaps, embody his happier vision of life in poetry, the fact that what he has left is the record of the struggle against doubt and despair should not obscure the evidence that Clough emerged from the struggle with a victory.

Clough's final position is not, after all, so different from that of Arnold. Arnold's acceptance of the inevitable pain of life is stoic and elegiac where Clough's is quietly trusting, but the rejection of all the shallower consolations of the Christian tradition exists in both. The strategy by which they imply rather than assert their hopes and faiths is also frequently the same: Clough's Jacob, sitting in his doorway in the evening, functions in the same way as the final descriptive stanzas of Arnold's "Obermann Once More." And, even though in his prose Arnold develops his beliefs much more fully than Clough ever did, his formulation of the power not ourselves that makes for righteousness is very close to the God Clough asks "The hand to sway, the judgment guide," for "Be thou but there,—in soul and heart,/I will not ask to feel thou art" (*Poems*, 88).

Arnold's statement that Clough was not an artist turns on the definition of the term. Clough was not an artist in the sense Arnold had in mind; he did not "group objects" (or concepts or sounds) with a view to producing a pleasing composition. (Nor did Arnold himself always regard the function of the artist so narrowly.) Clough perhaps even feared that a too-pleasing arrangement of language would corrode the honesty and accuracy of his analysis: in his as yet unpublished lecture on language he refers to the "perhaps *factitious opulence* of the English language." [23] But insofar as an "artist" is one able to express a response to life in such a way that the reader is able to understand and for the moment participate in that view, Clough may well claim the title. It is significant that the poetic record of these responses is most complete during the years of the greatest tension in the poet's mind, becoming more fragmentary as he moves toward a resolution and practically breaking off after it is achieved. Clough never regarded himself as a prophet whose duty it was to ascertain truth and promulgate it; his suspicion of the poet-as-prophet is expressed in the fragment "Poetry and Skepticism" in which he quotes from Xenophanes to the effect that no man may speak of the gods with certainty. Thus his poems record his struggle toward the resolution of certain problems, but they attempt no triumphant statement of that resolution.

III   *Twentieth-Century Revaluation*

The nineteenth century had a difficult time understanding a serious poet who would not assume the role of prophet, or at least of defender of certain values. Thus Patmore, the defender of the sanctities of domestic love, could make nothing of *Dipsychus*, the "tedious Mephistophelian drama . . . which Clough had the good sense not to publish." [24] Swinburne, although in his earlier poems the defender of things quite other than the domestic virtues championed so widely by his contemporaries, was also unable to find interest in a poet who was not promulgating *something*—especially a poet not dedicated to the creation of formal beauty. He had no use for Clough's "demi-semi-Christianity" or for "jungles of argument and brakes of analysis" in poetry, and dismissed him in a limerick: "There was a bad poet named Clough, whom his friends found it useless to puff: for the public, if dull, has not such a skull as belongs to believers in Clough." [25]

R. W. Church, who might have been expected—as a friend of

Clough's and as a churchman profoundly cognizant of the reasons
for and consequences of the turmoil within the Anglican Church
—to understand sympathetically Clough's position, was appalled
at the content of his poetry. After implying the possibility that
"unbelief is of itself the evidence and the result of something morally wrong at the foundation," Church lamented: "Alas! for those
who have no better guidance for immediate action than such as
they can obtain from the pages of Arthur Hugh Clough."[26] Edmund Gosse, carrying the Victorian predilection for banner-
carrying into the 1920's, complained that "Clough in later life
never led anybody anywhere," and he reminded his readers that
"Lord Morley is said to have refused to allow" Clough a place in
the English Men of Letters Series.[27]

But, as certain friends and admirers saw even in his own time,
Clough's poems have value precisely because he refused the role
of prophet and devoted himself to the careful and honest exploration of primary human questions. The value of his poetry lies in
the way it clarifies problems, even as it clarified them for Clough
himself, rather than in any answers it proposes, though Clough
did find an attitude toward life satisfactory for himself. It was to
that function of Clough's poetry, as well as to Clough's intellectual
integrity, that the philosopher Henry Sidgwick paid tribute in re-
cording, in 1870, his debt: "The truth is—if Clough had not lived
and written, I should probably be now exactly where he was.
I have not solved in any way the Gordian Knot which he fin-
gered. I can neither adequately rationalise faith, nor reconcile
faith and reason, nor suppress reason. But this is just the benefit of
an utterly veracious man like Clough, that it is impossible for any
one, however sympathetic, to remain where he was."[28]

Similarly, R. H. Hutton has described the important influence
of Clough on the mind of Walter Bagehot, the man G. M. Young
found to represent best the vigor and breadth of Victorian
thought.[29] According to Hutton, "Clough's chief fascination for
Bagehot was, I think, that he had as a poet in some measure redis-
covered, at all events realised, as few ever realised before, the
enormous difficulty of finding truth . . ." and Bagehot followed
Clough in guarding constantly against the mind's tendency to per-
suade itself into what it wishes to believe.

The last two decades have seen an increasing number of favorable critical revaluations of the worth of Clough's poetry, both in

itself and as a commentary on the mid-nineteenth century. Equally significant, and perhaps more interesting, are citations by Sir Winston Churchill and Graham Greene. It may be that a portion of the recent interest can be traced indirectly to Churchill's use of the closing two stanzas of "Say not the struggle" in his speech of April 27, 1941, to cheer the British people in the dark days before the entrance of the United States into the war. Churchill's choice of "Say not the struggle" was a tribute to the power of one of Clough's best-known poems.

A tribute to Clough's character is to be found in Graham Greene's *The Quiet American,* which carries as one of its epigraphs a passage from *Amours* expressing Claude's distrust of "our terrible notions of duty." Within the novel Thomas Fowler quotes six lines from *Dipsychus* which sum up his bitterness at the role played by the Americans in approving acts of terrorism and then offering money to the relatives of the victims: "And if I should chance to run over a cad,/I can pay for the damage if ever so bad." Fowler then comments that the author of the lines, whom he does not name, "was an adult poet in the nineteenth century. There weren't so many of them." [30] Within the context of the novel it is clear that Clough is seen as "adult" because of the honesty of his criticism both of himself and of the society around him.

Clough's intellectual honesty appears in his refusal to abandon his rigorous analysis of a problem until he had found an answer which satisfied him, in the lack of dogmatism with which he finally took his stand on those beliefs and hopes he could accept, and in the scrupulousness with which he recorded his intellectual strife in his poems. Whether or no his poems were an essential part of this analytical process, as has been argued here, there is never the slightest indication that the honesty with which they explore a possible position is compromised by a desire to produce a particular esthetic effect.

Clough's rare honesty manifests itself also in the complete lack of self-pity in his poems, even those in which he is exploring painful personal psychological reactions. No one could accuse him of being overly optimistic about the proportion between pain and happiness in the world nor of having had an unusually happy life, yet he saw no reason to indulge in expressions of despair about the evil of the world or in commiseration for himself. Nor apparently could he tolerate such a weakness in others—what he so strongly disliked in Sidney Walker's poetry was its strain of self-pity and "weak complaining cry."

One of the reasons Clough seems most to have valued the age of Dryden was its rigid intellectual honesty and avoidance of all illusion, including perhaps that of feeling oneself ill-used by the world. The sentence which Arnold delighted in quoting from Bishop Butler rang also in Clough's ears—"things and actions are what they are, and the consequences of them will be what they will be: why then should we desire to be deceived?" Perhaps there is no better way to close a study of Clough than to quote his praise for the spirit of the eighteenth century:

This austere love of truth; this righteous abhorrence of illusion; the rigorous uncompromising rejection of the vague, the untestified, the merely probable; this stern conscientious determination without paltering and prevarication to admit, if things are bad, that they are so; this resolute upright purpose as of some transcendental man of business, to go thoroughly into the accounts of the world and make out once for all how they stand, such a spirit, I may say, I think, claims more than our attention,—claims our reverence.[31]

Notes and References

Preface

1. *The Poems of Arthur Hugh Clough.* ed. H. F. Lowry, A. L. P. Norrington, and F. L. Mulhauser (Oxford, 1951). This edition is hereafter cited as Oxford *Poems.* See Gollin's "The 1951 Edition of Clough's Poems: A Critical Re-examination," *Modern Philology,* LX (Nov., 1962), 120–27.

Chapter One

1. James Russell Lowell, "Swinburne's Tragedies," in *My Study Windows* (Boston and New York, 1904 [Elmwood Edition]), p. 156.

2. Francis W. Palmer has discussed this point in "The Bearing of Science on the Thought of Arthur Hugh Clough," *PMLA,* LIX (Mar., 1944), 212–25.

3. See R. W. Church, *The Oxford Movement* (London, 1891), especially Chapter I.

4. John Keble, *The Oxford Movement Centenary: The Assize Sermon on "National Apostasy"* (London, 1931), p. 7.

5. See *Tracts for the Times,* 6 vols. (London and Oxford, 1834–1841).

6. See Chapter I, G. M. Young's *Victorian England* (London, 1936).

7. *The Correspondence of Arthur Hugh Clough,* ed. Frederick L. Mulhauser (Oxford, 1957), p. 180 (#147). Hereafter cited as *Correspondence.* Letter numbers are cited in parentheses after the page reference.

8. James Bertram has suggested that this poem may be identical with the "six more verses" Dipsychus promises his uncle at the end of the prose epilogue to *Dipsychus.* See *Review of English Studies,* n.s. VII (Jan., 1956), 59–60.

9. "Letters to Paripedemus, Number One," *Selected Prose Works of Arthur Hugh Clough,* ed. Buckner Trawick (University, Alabama, 1964), p. 176. Hereafter this voume will be cited as *Selected Prose.* I use the titles assigned by Professor Trawick whenever citing a prose work included in his edition.

10. Katharine Chorley: *Arthur Hugh Clough: The Uncommitted*

Mind (Oxford, 1962). Hereafter cited as Chorley. Paul Veyriras: *Arthur Hugh Clough* (Paris, 1964).

11. "Memoir," in *The Poems and Prose Remains of Arthur Hugh Clough* (London, 1869). Hereafter cited as the "Memoir."

12. Quoted in the Introduction to *The Letters of Matthew Arnold to Arthur Hugh Clough,* ed. H. F. Lowry (London and New York, 1932), p. 12.

13. James I. Osborne, *Arthur Hugh Clough* (Boston and New York, 1920), p. 29.

14. "Arthur Hugh Clough," in *The Eighteen-Sixties,* ed. John Drinkwater (London and New York, 1932), pp. 20–50.

15. Thomas Arnold, *Sermon Preached in the chapel of Rugby School* (London, 1845), pp. 66–74.

16. *Selected Prose,* p. 278.

17. See *Correspondence,* p. 12 (#9) and p. 48 (#28).

18. "Arthur Hugh Clough," in *An Old Castle and Other Essays* (New York, 1922), pp. 362–80.

19. *Correspondence,* p. 16 (#11).

20. *Ibid.,* pp. 45–46 (#28).

21. "Memoir," pp. 18–19.

22. *Ibid.,* p. 17.

23. Wilfred Ward, *W. G. Ward and the Oxford Movement* (London and Edinburgh, 1889), p. 110. Quoted in Chorley, p. 48.

24. *Correspondence,* p. 97 (#67).

25. *Ibid.,* pp. 80–83 (#53) and pp. 86–88 (#58).

26. *Edinburgh Review,* LXIII (Apr., 1836), 225–39.

27. *Correspondence,* p. 170 (#132).

28. Thomas Arnold, "Arthur Hugh Clough: A Sketch," *Nineteenth Century,* XLII (Jan., 1898), 112 and 115.

29. D. F. Strauss, *A New Life of Jesus* (London and Edinburgh, 1865 [Authorized Translation]), II, 435–36.

30. *Correspondence,* p. 182 (#149).

31. *Ibid.,* p. 249 (#214).

32. Bodleian Manuscript. M.S. Eng. lett. c.190. Letter #306. The numbering of the letters in the Bodleian collection corresponds with that of the "Catalogue of All Known Letters" in Vol. II of the *Correspondence.*

33. Chorley, p. 121.

34. *The Letters of Benjamin Jowett,* arranged and edited by Evelyn Abbott and Lewis Campbell (London, 1899), p. 177. Quoted in Chorley, p. 327.

35. Thomas Carlyle, *Heroes and Hero-Worship* (London, 1895 [Centenary Edition]), pp. 2–3.

36. Osborne, p. 112.

37. Thomas Carlyle, *Past and Present* (London, 1897 [Centenary Edition]), pp. 233–34.

38. *Correspondence*, p. 207 (#175).

39. *Selected Prose*, pp. 232–33.

40. These letters appear on pp. 273–76 of *Selected Prose* under the erroneous title "Two Letters about Francis W. Newman's *The Soul.*"

41. F. W. Newman, "On the Relation of Free Knowledge to Moral Sentiment" (London, 1847), pp. 5–6.

42. Robert H. Tener has pointed out that the Minute Book of University Hall indicates that Clough remained there until February, 1852. See "Clough, Hutton, and University Hall," *Notes and Queries*, n.s. VII (Dec., 1960), 456–57.

43. *Correspondence*, p. 301 (#261).

44. *Ibid.*, p. 300 (#260).

45. *Ibid.*, pp. 435–36 (#371).

46. Bodleian Manuscript. Eng. lett. c. 190. Letter #300, June 26, 1848.

47. *Ibid.* Letter #306, August 13, 1848.

48. Bodleian Manuscript. Eng. lett. d. 177. Letter #418, Sept. 14, 1851.

49. *DNB* (1909 edition), XXII:77.

50. *Correspondence*, pp. 248–49 (#214).

51. J. A. Froude, *The Nemesis of Faith* (London, 1849), p. 35.

52. See Edward Everett Hale, *J. R. Lowell and his Friends* (Boston and New York, 1899), p. 136.

53. Froude, *The Nemesis of Faith*, p. vi (see note 52 above).

Chapter Two

1. For Clough's account of the mishap of the name, see *Correspondence*, pp. 243–44 (#209), and p. 498 (#436).

2. *A History of English Prosody* (London, 1910), III, 408–10.

3. *English Tales in Verse* (London, 1902), p. lv.

4. *Milton's Prosody* together with W. J. Stone's *Classical Metres in English Verse* (Oxford, 1901), pp. 106–07.

5. "On Translating Homer," in *The Complete Prose Works of Matthew Arnold* (Ann Arbor, 1960 et seq.), I, 150.

6. George Saintsbury, *Historical Manual of English Prosody* (London, 1919), p. 257.

7. Charles Kingsley, "The Bothie of Toper-Na-Fuosich," *Fraser's Magazine*, XXXIX (Jan., 1849), 107. The attribution to Kingsley may be found in Thomas Arnold's "Arthur Hugh Clough," *Nineteenth Century*, XLIII (Jan., 1898), 109.

8. *Selected Prose*, p. 182.

9. Geoffrey Tillotson helpfully emphasizes the importance of this cardinal rule in "Clough's *Bothie*," *Mid-Victorian Studies* (London, 1965), pp. 118–44.

10. See "Dialogues on English Hexameters, No. II," *Fraser's Magazine,* XXXIX (Mar., 1849), 346.

11. Vol. XXXVI, 665–70; Vol. XXXIX, 342–47.

12. See R. W. Church's review in *The Christian Remembrancer,* XLV (Jan., 1863), 67.

13. Maurice Hewlett, "Teufelsdröckh in Hexameters," *Nineteenth Century,* XCI (Jan., 1922), 68–75.

14. Chorley, pp. 91–92.

15. Goldie Levy, *Arthur Hugh Clough* (London, 1938), p. 80.

16. Thomas Carlyle, *Sartor Resartus* (London, 1896 [Centenary Edition]), p. 107.

17. *Correspondence,* p. 243 (#209).

18. *Arthur Hugh Clough* (Boston and New York, 1920), pp. 54–55.

19. *Correspondence,* p. 240 (#206) and p. 247 (#213).

20. Clough replied to Hawkins that "I could wish several things altered." See *Correspondence,* p. 248 (#214). Clough's changes in the *Bothie* are conveniently indicated in *Poems of Clough,* ed. H. S. Milford (London, 1910).

21. "The Bothie of Toper-Na-Fuosich," p. 110 (see note 7 above).

Chapter Three

1. *Selected Prose,* p. 64.

2. Richard M. Gollin makes this point very well in "The 1951 Edition of Clough's Poems: A Critical Re-examination," *Modern Philology,* LX (Nov., 1962), 120–27. The four additional stanzas to "*Solvitur acris hiems*" first published and discussed by Evelyn Barish in "A New Clough Manuscript" (*Review of English Studies,* XV [ser. 2, May, 1964], 168–74) provide a good example.

3. See Samuel Waddington, *Arthur Hugh Clough* (London, 1883), p. 138.

4. *Correspondence,* p. 40 (# 24).

5. See the "Memoir," p. 35.

6. *Ibid.,* p. 25.

7. *Selected Prose,* p. 120.

8. "Memoir," p. 15.

9. See Richard Le Gallienne's "The Décadent to his Soul" in *English Poems* (London, 1892), pp. 106–09.

10. Chorley, pp. 92 and 242.

11. *Correspondence,* p. 141 (# 107).

12. Carlyle, *Sartor Resartus* (London, 1896 [Centenary Edition]), p. 127.

13. A convenient summary of a number of these reviews is to be found in Chorley, pp. 178–81.

Chapter Four

1. One short passage from *Amours* appears, with alterations, in *Dipsychus* (see pp. 204 and 240 of the Oxford *Poems*).

2. See *Correspondence*, pp. 252 ff.

3. From a letter to J. C. Shairp: "But do you not, in the conception, find any final strength of mind in the unfortunate fool of a hero? I have no intention of sticking up for him, but certainly I didn't mean him to go off into mere prostration and defeat." *Correspondence*, p. 278 (#238).

4. *Henry Sidgwick: A Memoir*, ed. Arthur and Eleanor M. Sidgwick (London, 1906), pp. 193–95.

5. Richard Gollin, "The 1951 Edition of Clough's Poems: A Critical Re-examination," *Modern Philology*, LX (Nov., 1962), p. 125.

6. Thomas Arnold, "Arthur Hugh Clough: A Sketch," *Nineteenth Century*, XLIII (June, 1898), 111.

7. See J. D. Jump, "Clough's *Amours de Voyage*," *English*, IX (Summer, 1953), 176–78; Michael Timko "*Amours de Voyage*: Substance or Smoke?" *English*, XIII (Autumn,1960), 95–98; V. S. Pritchett, "Books in General," *New Statesman and Nation*, XLI, series II (Jan. 6, 1951), 15–16.

Chapter Five

1. An interesting exception is the review in *Macmillan's Magazine*, XV (Dec., 1866), 89–102. Walter Houghton has discovered the author to have been William Henry Smith (see *The Poetry of Clough* [New Haven, 1963], p. 156n.).

2. A careful description of the various existing versions of *Dipsychus* is given in the notes to the Oxford *Poems*, pp. 528 ff.

3. Chorley, pp. 264–66.

4. *Correspondence*, pp. 283–84 (#243).

5. *Selected Prose*, p. 281.

6. Walter Bagehot, *Literary Studies* (London, 1895), II, 264.

7. *Goethe's Faust with a New Translation and Introduction by Walter Kaufmann* (Garden City, 1961), p. 133. Copyright (C) 1961 by Walter Kaufmann. Reprinted by permission of Doubleday and Company, Inc.

Chapter Six

1. These datings are derived primarily from the very helpful notes on the manuscript and printed versions of each poem provided in the Oxford *Poems*.

2. See "Memoirs," pp. 44–45.

3. *Correspondence*, p. 364 (#326).

4. *Ibid.*, p. 371 (#331).

5. *Ibid.*, p. 411 (355).

6. See Note 30 to Chapter I.

7. *Selected Prose*, p. 291.

8. See volume on "Genesis" of the *International Critical Commentary on the Holy Scriptures* . . . , ed. S. R. Driver, *et al.* (Edinburgh, 1930 [2nd ed.]), p. 122.

9. Oxford *Poems*, p. 276.

10. *Selected Prose*, p. 118.

11. Paul Veyriras argues that the sonnet printed as the fourth in the Oxford edition but which occupies the sixth place in the MS. ought to be printed as the sixth sonnet and that the six lines beginning "But that from slow dissolving pomps of dawn" (p. 395 of the Oxford edition) were intended as a conclusion to sonnet III. *Arthur Hugh Clough* (Paris, 1964), pp. 317–18.

12. *Selected Prose*, p. 282.

13. *Ibid.*, p. 138.

14. *Ibid.*, p. 280.

15. *Ibid.*, p. 286.

16. See the Oxford *Poems*, p. 240.

17. A very interesting discussion of this poem, which suggests among other things that Clough was in part parodying Isaac Watts's versified children's version of the Ten Commandments, is P. G. Scott's "The Text and Structure of Clough's 'The Latest Decalogue,'" *Notes and Queries*, CCXII (Oct., 1967), 378–79.

18. *Selected Prose*, p. 145.

19. *Correspondence*, pp. 400–02 (#348) and p. 444 (#382).

20. *Ibid.*, p. 460 (#399).

Chapter Seven

1. It is of course true that Clough had certain general attitudes about the content of poetry; these have been well explored in Michael Timko's "The Poetic Theory of Arthur Hugh Clough," *English Studies*, XLIII (1962), pp. 240–47.

2. *Selected Prose*, p. 31.

3. *Ibid.*, pp. 226–27.

4. *Ibid.*, pp. 119, 121, and 122.

5. *Ibid.*, p. 168.
6. *Ibid.*, p. 210.
7. *Ibid.*, p. 211.
8. *Ibid.*, p. 217.
9. *Ibid.*, p. 225.
10. *Ibid.*, p. 233.
11. *Ibid.*, p. 242.
12. *Ibid.*, p. 251.
13. *Ibid.*, pp. 252–53.
14. *Ibid.*, pp. 230-31.
15. *Ibid.*, pp. 244–45.
16. *Ibid.*, p. 246.
17. *Ibid.*, p. 223.
18. *Ibid.*, pp. 262–63.
19. *Ibid.*, p. 265.
20. *Ibid.*, p. 279.
21. *Correspondence*, p. 398 (#347).
22. *Selected Prose*, p. 288.
23. *Ibid.*, p. 279.
24. *Correspondence*, p. 427 (#363).
25. *Selected Prose*, p. 289.
26. *Ibid.*, pp. 289–90. Carlyle makes much the same point in *Sartor Resartus* (London, 1896 [Centenary Edition]), p. 154–55.
27. *Ibid.*, pp. 290–91.
28. *Ibid.*, p. 290.
29. *Ibid.*, p. 292.
30. *Ibid.*, p. 293.
31. Bodleian Manuscript. Eng. misc. d. 512, fols. 165–66.

Chapter Eight

1. See A. M. Turner, "A Study of Clough's *Mari Magno*," *PMLA*, XLIV (June, 1929), 569–89.
2. "Memoir," p. 10.
3. *Correspondence*, p. 522 (#463).
4. See Levy, *Arthur Hugh Clough*, p. 167.
5. Quoted in Chorley, p. 263.
6. Oxford *Poems*, p. 195.
7. 'Memoir," pp. 41 and 48.

Chapter Nine

1. Lionel Trilling, *Matthew Arnold* (New York and London, 1949), p. 23.
2. *Unpublished Letters of Matthew Arnold*, ed. Arnold Whitridge (New Haven, 1923), p. 17.

3. See *The Letters of Matthew Arnold to Arthur Hugh Clough,* ed. H. F. Lowry (London and New York, 1932), pp. 130, 157, 159.

4. *Ibid.,* p. 63.

5. *Ibid.,* p. 64.

6. *Ibid.,* p. 84.

7. *Ibid.,* p. 129.

8. *Ibid.,* p. 95.

9. *Ibid.,* p. 99.

10. *Correspondence,* p. 307 (#274).

11. *Selected Prose,* pp. 96–97.

12. *Ibid.,* p. 114.

13. *The Letters of Matthew Arnold to Arthur Hugh Clough,* p. 130.

14. *Ibid.,* p. 146.

15. Roger L. Brooks has pointed out in "Matthew Arnold's Revision of Tristram and Iseult: Some Instances of Clough's Influence" (*Victorian Poetry,* II [Winter, 1964], 57–60) that Arnold apparently revised *Tristram and Iseult* for his *Poems* (1853) with the strictures of Clough's review in mind.

16. *Selected Prose,* p. 153.

17. *Ibid.,* p. 165.

18. *Correspondence,* p. 424 (#361).

19. *Ibid.,* p. 301 (#262).

20. *The Letters of Matthew Arnold to Arthur Hugh Clough,* p. 126.

21. See Paul Turner, " 'Dover Beach' and *The Bothie of Tober-na-Vuolich,*" *English Studies,* XXVII (Dec., 1947), 173–78; Buckner Trawick, "The Sea of Faith and the Battle by Night in 'Dover Beach,' " *PMLA,* LXV (Dec., 1950), 1282–83; David Robertson, " 'Dover Beach' and 'Say Not the Struggle Nought Availeth,' " *PMLA,* LXVI (Dec., 1951), 919–28; W. Stacy Johnson, "Parallel Imagery in Arnold and Clough," *English Studies,* XXXVII (Feb., 1956), 1–11. Paull F. Baum has argued against Robertson's view in "Clough and Arnold," *Modern Language Notes,* LXVII (Dec., 1952), 546–47, as has Harry W. Rudman in *Notes and Queries,* CXCVIII (June, 1953), 261–63.

22. Johnson's other example of Clough's use of the image of a ship bound for an uncertain port is drawn from a series of similar poems sent to Blanche from America, and, obviously suggested by Clough's own voyage, intended to express, most probably, the practical difficulties lying between him and marriage to Blanche.

23. Bodleian Manuscript. Eng. misc. d. 511, p. 216. Italics mine.

24. *Principle in Art* (London, 1912), p. 89.

25. *The Complete Works of Algernon Charles Swinburne* (London and New York, 1926 [Bonchurch Edition]), XV, 22, 71, and 283.

26. Review of Clough's *Poems* in the *Christian Rememrancer*, XLV (Jan., 1863), 88.

27. Edmund Gosse, *Books on the Table* (London, 1921), pp. 130 and 129.

28. *Henry Sidgwick: A Memoir*, ed. Arthur and Eleanor M. Sidgwick (London, 1906), p. 227.

29. See R. H. Hutton, "Walter Bagehot," *Fortnightly Review*, XXVIII (Oct., 1877), 466–69. G. M. Young, "The Greatest Victorian," *Spectator*, CLVIII (June, 1937), 1137–38, and "The Case for Walter Bagehot," *Spectator*, CLIX (July, 1937), 9–10. For Clough's influence on Bagehot, see also Alastair Buchan, *The Spare Chancellor* (London, 1959), pp. 48–54.

30. London, 1955, pp. 31–32. Harry W. Rudman was the first to call attention to these references; see "Clough and Graham Greene," *Victorian Newsletter*, No. 19 (Spring, 1961), 14–15.

31. *Selected Prose*, p. 137.

Selected Bibliography

PRIMARY SOURCES

1. *The most important of Clough's writings published during his life-time.*

Seventeen poems and thirteen prose articles published in the *Rugby Magazine*, 2 Vols. (1835–37). A list of these contributions is provided by Isobel Armstrong in: *Arthur Hugh Clough*. London: Longman, 1962 (Writers and their Work Series).

Six letters to *The Balance* (London). Letter to the Editor (Jan. 23, 1846, p. 26); "Political Economy" (Jan. 30, 1846, p. 34); "The Militia" (Feb. 6, 1846, p. 42); "Expensive Living" (Feb. 13, 1846, p. 50); "A Few Practical Hints" (Mar. 6, 1848, p. 77); "The Spirit of Trade" (Mar. 20, 1846, pp. 93–94).

"A Consideration of Objections against the Retrenchment Association." Oxford: Francis MacPherson, 1847.

The Bothie of Toper-na-Fuosich: A Long Vacation Pastoral. Oxford: Francis MacPherson; and London: Chapman and Hall, 1848 (Afterward *The Bothie of Tober-na-Vuolich*).

Ambarvalia: Poems by T. Burbidge and A. H. Clough. London and Oxford: Chapman and Hall, 1849.

"Recent English Poetry," *North American Review*, LXXVII (July, 1853), 1–30. A review of Alexander Smith's *Poems*, Matthew Arnold's *The Strayed Reveller* and *Empedocles on Etna*, William Sidney Walker's *Poetic Remains*, and William Allingham's *Poems*.

"Recent Social Theories," *North American Review*, LXXVII (July, 1853), 106–17. A review of Charles Eliot Norton's *Considerations on Some Recent Social Theories*.

Amours de Voyage. Serial publication in the *Atlantic Monthly*, I (Feb.-May, 1858).

"Poems and Ballads of Goethe," *Fraser's Magazine*, LIX (June, 1859), 710–17. A review of *Poems and Ballads of Goethe*, trans. W. E. Aytoun, D. C. and T. Martin.

Plutarch's Lives. The translation called Dryden's, corrected from the Greek and revised by A. H. Clough, 5 vols. Boston, 1859.

2. *The most important collections of Clough's writings published after his death.*

Poems. Cambridge: Macmillan and Co., 1862, with a Memoir by F. T. Palgrave. Boston: Ticknor and Fields, 1862, with an Introduction by C. E. Norton.

The Poems and Prose Remains of Arthur Hugh Clough. With a selection from his Letters and a Memoir [largely by Blanche Clough]. Edited by his wife with J. A. Symonds. 2 vols. London: Macmillan and Co., 1869.

The Poems of A. H. Clough. Ed. H. F. Lowry, A. L. P. Norrington, and F. L. Mulhauser. Oxford: Clarendon Press, 1951.

The Correspondence of A. H. Clough. Ed. F. L. Mulhauser. 2 vols. Oxford: Clarendon Press, 1957. Includes letters originally published as *The Emerson-Clough Letters,* ed. H. F. Lowry and R. L. Rusk. Cleveland, 1934.

Selected Prose Works of Arthur Hugh Clough. Ed. Buckner B. Trawick. University, Alabama: University of Alabama Press, 1964.

A Selection from Arthur Hugh Clough. Ed. John Purkis. London: Longmans, 1967. Annotated selection with helpful commentary.

SECONDARY SOURCES

1. *Bibliographies*

EHRSAM, T. G. and R. H. DEILY. *Bibliographies of Twelve Victorian Authors.* New York: H. W. Wilson, 1936. List of articles and books about Clough and reviews of his poetry. Supplemented by J. G. Fucilla in *Modern Philology,* XXXVII (Aug., 1939), 89–96.

GOLLIN, RICHARD M., WALTER E. HOUGHTON, and MICHAEL TIMKO. "Arthur Hugh Clough: A Descriptive Catalogue," *Bulletin of the New York Public Library,* LXX (Nov., 1966), 554–85 [Part I, Poetry]; LXXI (Jan., 1967), 55–58 [Part II, Prose Supplement]; LXXI (Feb., Mar., 1967), 71–92, 173–99 [Part III, Biography and Criticism]. Rptd. in a single volume, including Houghton checklist, under the same title by the New York Public Library, 1967. Supersedes all other bibliographies of Clough. Very helpful annotations.

HOUGHTON, W. E. "The Prose Works of Arthur Hugh Clough: A Checklist and a Calendar. . . ," *The Bulletin of the New York Public Library,* LXIV (July, 1960), 377–94.

2. Biography and Criticism

ALLINGHAM, WILLIAM. "Arthur Hugh Clough, 1819–61," *Fraser's Magazine*, LXXIV (Oct., 1866), 525–35. A general biographical and appreciative account; valuable for those without convenient access to Mrs. Clough's "Memoir"—from which it is largely drawn.

ARNOLD, THOMAS. "Arthur Hugh Clough: A Sketch," *Nineteenth Century*, XLIII (June, 1898), 105–16. Rptd. in Arnold's *Passages in a Wandering Life*. London: Edward Arnold, 1900. Arnold's memories of Clough; valuable for biographical details.

BAGEHOT, WALTER. "Mr. Clough's Poems," *National Review*, XV (Oct. 1862), 310–26. Rptd. in his *Literary Studies*. Vol. II. London: Longmans, 1879. One of the most perceptive and frequently cited contemporary reviews of Clough's works.

BARISH, EVELYN. "A New Clough Manuscript," *Review of English Studies*, n.s. XV (May, 1964), 167–74. Four additional stanzas of "Solvitur acris hiems" together with an incisive discussion of the total poem.

BOWERS, FREDERICK. "Arthur Hugh Clough: The Modern Mind," *Studies in English Literature*, VI (Autumn, 1966), 709–16. Good discussion of the modernity of Clough's verse.

BOWERS, FREDERICK. "Arthur Hugh Clough: Recent Revaluations," *Humanities Association Bulletin* (of Canada), XVI (Fall, 1965), 17–26. A good general survey of Clough editions and scholarship to the time of writing.

BROOKE, STOPFORD A. *Four Poets*. London: Duckworth and Co., 1908. Rather romantic treatment of Clough's quest for truth.

CHORLEY, LADY KATHARINE. *Arthur Hugh Clough: The Uncommitted Mind*. Oxford and New York: Clarendon Press, 1962. Most complete biography of Clough. Somewhat psychoanalytical in its interpretations.

[CHURCH, R. W.] Review of the *Bothie, Ambarvalia*, and *Poems* in *The Christian Remembrancer*, XLV (Jan., 1863), 61–89. Very interesting as an example of the frequent depreciations of Clough in the middle of the nineteenth century.

COCKSHUT, A. O. J. "Clough: The Real Doubter." *The Unbelievers*. New York: New York University Press, 1966. Defense of the sincerity of Clough's doubts and the clearness of his thinking.

"Dialogues on English Hexameters, No. II," *Fraser's Magazine*, XXXIX (Mar., 1849), 342–47. Interesting analysis of Clough's hexameters in the *Bothie*.

GOLLIN, RICHARD M. "The 1951 Edition of Clough's Poems: A Critical Re-examination," *Modern Philology*, LX (Nov., 1962), 120–

127. Important in pointing out the deficiencies of the 1951 Oxford *Poems*.

GOSSE, EDMUND. *Books on the Table*. London: Heinemann, 1921. The chapter on Clough represents the strongest judgment of Clough as a failure.

HEWLETT, MAURICE. "Teufelsdröckh in Hexameters," *Nineteenth Century*, XCI, (Jan. 1922), 68–75. A novel appreciation of the *Bothie*.

HOUGHTON, WALTER E. *The Poetry of Clough*. New Haven and London: Yale University Press, 1963. Fullest defense of Clough as poet.

HUTTON, RICHARD HOLT. "Arthur Hugh Clough," *Spectator*, XLII (Sept., 1869), 1073–75. Rptd. with changes in: *Essays Theological and Literary*. Vol. II. London: Strahan and Co., 1871. Also rptd.: *Literary Essays*. London and New York: Longmans, 1892. Defense of Clough's poetry and favorable comparison with Matthew Arnold.

JOHNSON, WENDELL STACY. "Parallel Imagery in Arnold and Clough," *English Studies*, XXXVII (Feb., 1956), 1–11. On the poetic "debate" between Arnold and Clough. Sums up earlier articles on the subject.

[KINGSLEY, CHARLES.] "The Bothie of Toper-na-Fuosich," *Fraser's Magazine*, XXXIX (Jan., 1849), 103–10. Very high praise of the *Bothie*.

LEVY, GOLDIE. *Arthur Hugh Clough*. London: Sidgwick and Jackson, 1938. Workmanlike biography.

LOWRY, HOWARD FOSTER. *The Letters of Matthew Arnold to Arthur Hugh Clough*. London and New York: Oxford University Press, 1932. The letters are crucial for an understanding of the relationship between Arnold and Clough; the Introduction is excellent.

McCARTHY, DESMOND. *Portraits*. London: Putnam and Co., 1931. Essay on Clough challenges the image created by Lytton Strachey in *Eminent Victorians*.

MILFORD, HUMPHREY S. Introduction. *Poems of Clough*. London: Henry Froude, 1910. Analyses and defense of Clough's hexameters.

MIYOSHI, MASAO. "Clough's Poems of Self-Irony," *Studies in English Literature*, V (Autumn, 1965), 691–704. An examination of Clough's irony and satire, especially in relationship to the Romantic poets.

OSBORNE, JAMES I. *Arthur Hugh Clough*. Boston: Houghton, Mifflin, 1920. A biography which remains valuable for its critical commentary.

PALMER, FRANCIS W. "The Bearing of Science on the Thought of Arthur Hugh Clough," *PMLA*, LIX (Mar., 1944), 212–25. Discussion of Clough's scientific attitude in trusting only to facts.

PRITCHETT, V. S. "Books in General," *New Statesman and Nation,* XLI, ser. 2 (Jan. 6, 1951), 15–16. Refreshing revaluation of *Amours.*

ROBERTSON, JOHN MACKINNON. *New Essays Toward a Critical Method.* London and New York: John Lane, 1897. Essay on Clough argues that *Bothie* and *Amours* analyze character in a way that is an advance on fiction of Clough's time.

RYALS, CLYDE DE L. "An Interpretation of Clough's *Dipsychus,*" *Victorian Poetry,* I (Aug., 1963), 182–88. Reading of the poem which sees both Dipsychus and the Spirit as incomplete without the other.

SIDGWICK, HENRY. "The Poems and Prose Remains of Arthur Hugh Clough." *Westminster Review,* XCII (Oct., 1869), 175–86. Rptd. in: *Miscellaneous Essays and Addresses.* London: Macmillan and Co. 1904. Very perceptive review which sees world coming more and more to point of view held by Clough.

SYMONDS, J. A. "Arthur Hugh Clough," *Fortnightly,* X (Dec., 1868), 589–617. Favorable review of the bulk of Clough's poetry. Comments on Clough's understanding of the necessity of breaking through the "metaphysical husks" around the religion of his time.

TIMKO, MICHAEL. *Innocent Victorian: The Satiric Poetry of Arthur Hugh Clough.* Athens, Ohio: Ohio University Press, 1966. Argues that Clough "did achieve a religious philosophy that was for him practically useful and deeply satisfying" and that critics have underestimated the extent of Clough's satiric vision. Includes an analysis of Clough's poetic theory.

TURNER, ALBERT M. "A Study of Clough's *Mari Magno,*" *PMLA,* XLIV (June, 1929), 569–89. Discusses Clough's use of his own experiences in *Mari Magno.*

VEYRIRAS, PAUL. *Arthur Hugh Clough.* Paris: 1964. (*Etudes Anglaises,* 22). A very thorough critical biography containing close analysis of Clough's intellectual stance, versification, and relation to the thought and movement of the time.

WADDINGTON, SAMUEL. *Arthur Hugh Clough.* London: Bell, 1883. Uncritical, but shows Clough from perspective of a nineteenth-century admirer.

WAUGH, ARTHUR. *Reticence in Literature and Other Papers.* London: Wilson, 1913. The essay "The Poetry of Reflection and Doubt" compares the outlook of Clough with that of Matthew Arnold; Arnold turned to the "life of ideas," Clough to the "life of humanity."

WOLFE, HUMBERT. "Arthur Hugh Clough." *The Eighteen-Sixties.* Ed. John Drinkwater. New York: Macmillan, 1932. Clough seen as "smothered by Arnoldism."

Index

It was not felt necessary to index the prefatory material, bibliography, or, with the exception of explanatory references, the notes to the text. Titles of works mentioned will be found listed under authors' names.